Cambridge Elements

Elements in the History of Philosophy and Theology in the West
edited by
Alexander J. B. Hampton
University of Toronto

THE METAPHYSICS OF DIVINE PARTICIPATION

Alexander J. B. Hampton
University of Toronto and University of Notre Dame Australia

Shaftesbury Road, Cambridge CB2 8EA, United Kingdom

One Liberty Plaza, 20th Floor, New York, NY 10006, USA

477 Williamstown Road, Port Melbourne, VIC 3207, Australia

314–321, 3rd Floor, Plot 3, Splendor Forum, Jasola District Centre, New Delhi – 110025, India

103 Penang Road, #05–06/07, Visioncrest Commercial, Singapore 238467

Cambridge University Press is part of Cambridge University Press & Assessment, a department of the University of Cambridge.

We share the University's mission to contribute to society through the pursuit of education, learning and research at the highest international levels of excellence.

www.cambridge.org
Information on this title: www.cambridge.org/9781009625043

DOI: 10.1017/9781009625036

When citing this work, please include a reference to the DOI 10.1017/9781009625036

First published 2025

A catalogue record for this publication is available from the British Library

ISBN 978-1-009-62504-3 Hardback
ISBN 978-1-009-62508-1 Paperback
ISSN 3033-3954 (online)
ISSN 3033-3946 (print)

The Metaphysics of Divine Participation

Elements in the History of Philosophy and Theology in the West

DOI: 10.1017/9781009625036
First published online: April 2025

Alexander J. B. Hampton
University of Toronto and University of Notre Dame Australia

Author for correspondence: Alexander J. B. Hampton, a.hampton@utoronto.ca

Abstract: Participation has been central to the story of Western philosophy and theology for at least two millennia. It has been employed to conceptualise the relationship between God and creation, between universals and particulars, and between the One and the many. This Element approaches the concept systematically to acquire an appreciation of its breadth and depth under four fundamental themes: creation and the divine ideas, incarnation and salvation, being and multiplicity, and the human activities of naming, knowing and making. In doing so it examines some of the key thinkers in the participatory tradition, including Augustine, Irenaeus, Aquinas, and Nicholas of Cusa. Readers will be introduced to the key contours and manifestations of participatory metaphysics, and its role in Christianity's self-articulation. Together, these considerations will demonstrate how the metaphysics of participation has shaped the Christian tradition.

Keywords: participation, Christianity, metaphysics, theology, philosophy

ISBNs: 9781009625043 (HB), 9781009625081 (PB), 9781009625036 (OC)
ISSNs: 3033-3954 (online), 3033-3946 (print)

Contents

1 The Metaphysics of Divine Participation

At first mention, participation might seem to be a simple relational concept. However, as is the case with so many fundamental and ostensibly familiar concepts, we find that it is also puzzling and complex. When we think of participation, we often think of taking part, as the English word itself suggests to us. One of the first things that might come to mind is group participation. We might be part of a team, and as part of that team, we might participate in a match. We may also participate in other broader or somewhat more abstract concepts. We can participate in the life of our community, through civil and religious bodies. Beyond this there are other forms of participation of which we have less, or even no, control over. We participate in a global economy whose complexity is difficult to conceive, yet whose breadth is difficult not to take part in. Still further, we participate by necessity in our environment, which we both affect and which effects us, and from which we cannot separate ourselves. These are forms of participation which may, upon reflection, be familiar to us.

This study focuses on a particular metaphysical understanding of participation that is found in the Western intellectual tradition, and in Christianity specifically. This stands alongside other traditions of participation found in other forms of Christianity, and in other religious and spiritual traditions.[1] The purpose of metaphysics is to account for the nature of reality itself, and in particular its most fundamental structure at the level of being (or existence). Under this definition of metaphysics, all individuals hold their own metaphysical position whether implicitly or explicitly. In the sense that we hold there to be a fundamental structure to reality, reflected upon or not, whether that structure be physical and made of atoms, or metaphysical and reliant upon the goodness of God, or some other conceptualisation. The role of participation then, in this metaphysical context, is to conceptualise the relationship between this more fundamental reality, and the particularity of the world in which we live. In this way, we should understand the concept of participation that will be examined here as neither strictly a philosophy nor a theology. Instead, participation is a concept that is key to many doctrines in theology, such as incarnation, creation, salvation, and many more. Furthermore, it is fundamentally present in

[1] For examples see contributions to *The Participatory Turn: Spirituality, Mysticism, Religious Studies*, ed. Jorge N. Ferrer and Jacob H. Sherman (Albany: State University of New York Press, 2008): Jorge N. Ferrer, 'Spiritual Knowing as Participatory Enaction: An Answer to the Question of Religious Pluralism', 135–72; Brian L. Lancaster, 'Engaging with the Mind of God: The Participatory Path of Jewish Mysticism', 173–97; William C. Chittick, 'Ibn al-'Arabī on Participating in the Mystery', 245–64; Donald Rothberg, 'Connecting Inner and Outer Transformation: Toward an Extended Model of Buddhist Practice', 349–70.

philosophy, in the forms of metaphysics, epistemology, and ethics that are touched upon in this text.

The notion of participation naturally arises from basic, even simple, questions we have about the nature of reality and the source of meaning in our world. Since participation in the context of Christianity is fundamentally about the relationship between God and creation, it is not enough to examine the sources and identify instances of the word itself. As a relational concept, it is not reducible to its technical articulation alone. There are many instances where conceptually the notion of participation is key, but it is not named as such in an explicit way. This poses a challenge for any endeavor such as the one undertaken in this text. However, it is also an opportunity in that it allows us to see the broad use of a concept across numerous figures and periods.

The metaphysics of divine participation is a notion that is best approached contextually, through its particular manifestations, as they relate to fundamental questions, and systematically, to acquire an appreciation of its breadth and depth. This introductory examination will examine some of the primary manifestations in the sections that follow, exploring some of the ways in which the metaphysics of participation shaped and continues to shape the Christian tradition, generating a fascinating set of concepts and patterns that have been central to the story of Western philosophy and theology for at least two millennia.

Participation in Context

Section 1 provides a general overview of the concept, offering an initial definition, which places participation in a broader conceptual and historical context. The remaining sections take up central theological and philosophical themes in the metaphysics of participation, with each section drawing upon the thought of a key representative figure from either the ancient or medieval world, and often additionally the thought of a modern figure, to explicate that theme. This has the benefit of approaching participation thematically, whilst also offering historical highlights in its development.

Section 2 takes up the foundational theme of creation. Creation is the place where participation occurs, and without participation there is no creation. This section looks at the origins of the concept of participation and its relation to the notion of divine ideas, first in Plato, and then through its adoption and modification into Christian thought in Augustine via Philo. In Augustine's Christianised version of participation, we see the development of a notion of the inherent goodness of creation which would be central for the further development of Christian participatory metaphysics.

Section 3 relates participation to the figure of Jesus Christ, and focuses upon the incarnation and salvation, and the participatory framework through which these are conceptualised by Irenaeus of Lyon. Irenaeus understands the condition of participation as one of continuous becoming. This becoming occurs in the context of the divine economy, where the incarnation opens the possibility for human beings to restore the post-lapsarian condition to ever greater levels of participation in the image and likeness of God, as made possible through the incarnation. In this way, we see Irenaeus setting out an understanding of human participation that is deeply personal whilst simultaneously placing it within a broader history of the creation, fall, incarnation and salvation. The notion of incarnation and salvation as the participatory drama of human beings is further elaborated in this section by turning to Hans Urs von Balthasar.

The consideration of creation, and then incarnation and salvation, build towards the topic of being, take up in Section 4. This section focuses upon the thought of Aquinas, perhaps the most important element of the metaphysics of divine participation, the participation of creatures in both being and essence, is taken up. In particular, it traces out Aquinas' important reformulation of the notion of the divine ideas in relation to the concepts of creatio ex nihilo, continuous creation, and analogy. Furthermore, it considers the importance of multiplicity in creation as a form of divine revelation. The notion of the analogy of being, that existence itself is an ontological analogy of the divine, is considered in the thought of Erich Przywara.

Section 5 examines participation from a particularly human-sided perspective. Through the lens of Nicholas of Cusa, it considers how the activities of naming, knowing, and making are fundamentally participatory, in that they are ways in which human beings directly and purposively engage in a participatory relationship with God and creation. In this section, special attention is given to the role of art as a form of human participation in the divine in the context of Romantic aesthetics and the thought of Friedrich Schlegel and Samuel Taylor Coleridge.

Defining Participation

The intention behind this study of participation is to allow for an understanding of the concept to emerge out of the contextual manifestations covered in these sections. Any essentialist definition of the concept runs the risk of falling afoul of the situational nature of the relational character of the concept. Nevertheless, it would undoubtedly be disappointing to the reader of this text if some definition was not proffered here in the introduction before the complexities and nuances of participation are brought out in the sections that follow. This is best accomplished by outlining a set of characteristics that arise out of the nature of the concept itself.

Relation

The purpose, and therefore the general meaning, of the notion of participation arises initially out of a basic fact of experience that gives rise to a philosophical question. This is the need to explain how it is that multiple subjects possess a common attribute, and to answer that question by reference to a higher source from which they receive, or participate in, the attribute which they possess in a common yet diminished form. In more basic terms, it is a relation for rendering intelligible a group (or 'many') which shares a common attribute in relation to a higher source (or 'One'), whether logical or ontological. It has therefore been used in different contexts to explain how all particular beings share in the same transcendental perfection of existence that is received from a supreme source in God, how multiple specific forms share in the same genus, and how all the members of a particular species share in the form of that species. Consequently, at its core participation is a relationship that adheres between two constituents.

The relationship between God and creation can further be understood in terms of the relation between universals and particulars, or the One and the many. God's unique nature ensures that the God–creature relationship is unlike any other form of relationship that adheres between creatures themselves. This is expressed in the radical asymmetry of the relationship, wherein the existence of creatures is entirely dependent upon the creator, and the existence of God is entirely independent of creatures. God is ontologically prior to creation, and all creatures that make up creation exist in a state of non-reciprocal dependence upon God, both for their existence and for their particularity, as is detailed further in Sections 2 and 4. This is put succinctly by Aquinas: 'God is being by his own essence, because he is the very act of being. Every other being, however, is a being by participation . . . . God, therefore, is the cause of being to all other things'.[2]

Immanence and Transcendence

Creatures are transcended by God upon whom they depend for their very existence. However, this transcendence is not merely a matter of creation, as the sections that follow will detail. It is also the matter of an ongoing

[2] All quotations from *Summa contra Gentiles* are from the edition translated by Anton C. Pegis, et al. 4 vols. (Notre Dame: University of Notre Dame Press, 1975), II.15.5.

relationship. Creaturely reality requires divine presence if it is to come to be and sustain itself. Consequently, creatures are more than just dependent upon God; they are also manifestations and reflections of the divine. In this way God is immanent in creation, whilst at the same time, by virtue of the transcendent asymmetry of the participatory relationship, never circumscribed or limited by creation. In participatory metaphysics divine transcendence and immanence exist together, not as opposites, but as dependents. On the one hand, God is not part of the larger whole of creation; God transcends creation. On the other hand, God is immanent in creation, present and manifest in every individual creature. In the context of Christian metaphysics, this is neither pantheistic nor panentheistic, since the God of Genesis creates ex nihilo, out of nothing. This marks out a fundamental distinction between God and creation, such that God is not continuous with creation, much the same way that an artist is not part of their artwork. The upshot of this distinction is that God and creatures cannot be compared or contrasted, as if they were part of the same species. Immanence and transcendence are not in opposition, but complementary ways in which the participatory relationship may be understood.

Revelation

In the context of Christianity, this participatory relationship unfolds in two broad forms which may be termed general and specific (or alternatively strong and weak).[3] In the general sense, which is considered in greater detail in Sections 2 and 4, all of creation is understood as having its source in the creator God, and having continued existence through the continuous act of divine creation. In this general sense, all things in creation, both human and otherwise, have their existence and their particular qualities by virtue of their participation in God. In the specific sense, creation is not only shaped by God's act of creation, but also by God's becoming incarnate and participating in the life of humanity more directly, as explored in Section 3. This act in history opens the possibility of salvation and redemption, and introduces an element of voluntary participation on the part of individual humans beyond the general participatory relationship already outlined. This distinction between general and specific corresponds, mutatis mutandis, to that sometimes made in Christianity between general and special forms of revelation. In general revelation, God is understood to be revealed through creation in general, and made accessible through natural reason and wonder. Special revelation is a particular historical revelation to

[3] Louis-Bertrand Geiger, *La participation dans la philosophie de St. Thomas d'Aquin* (Paris: J. Vrin, 1942), 11 ff.

a selected group of people, the examples of this being prophecy and the ministry of Jesus Christ, as recorded in scripture. Christianity has a longstanding debate as to whether, and to what extent, general revelation is possible without special revelation. For the purposes of this study, it is sufficient that we recognise these two forms of revelation as connected by participation.

Sharing

The participatory relationship is fundamentally one of sharing. We can see this by examining the etymology of the word. The Greek word μέθεξις/*méthexis* is first used in a metaphysical context by Plato to express the relationship between concepts and their predicates, ideas in their instantiations, or universals and their particular manifestations.[4] Plato does not use the term in a technical sense, and states that it should not be used as such[5]; perhaps to reenforce this, he employs a multiplicity of other terms to express it.[6] The prefix of the word means 'among' or 'with', whilst the root of the word means to 'share in'. Together the word connotes 'being after' in a successive sense, as well as 'following' or 'pursuing' in a dynamic sense.[7] Consequently, if something participates in the metaphysical context of Plato's thought, it has its reality both after and in pursuit of a form specifically, or the Good in general. This Greek context differentiates the metaphysical use of the term from the modern English sense that its translation via Latin (participatio) into participation carries. This modern sense suggests taking a part, in the sense of appropriating that which previously belonged to another, and the divisibility that accompanies this conceptualisation. However, the metaphysical sense of participation that is examined here is not the reception of a part of something else. Instead, it is better understood as becoming a partner or participant in something shared. Aquinas himself, working in Latin, seems to have begun with this problematic understanding of participation as connoting division, and then in the course of his own theological development, came to arrive at an

---

4 Sr. M. Annice, 'Historical Sketch of the Theory of Participation', *New Scholasticism*, 26 (1952): 49–79, here: 51. Evangelos Moutsopoulos supplies some key references to Plato's use of the term in 'L'Idée de participation: Cosmos et praxis', *Philosophia*, 32 (2002): 17–21: Protagoras 322a; Symposium 208b; Republic VI 486a; Parmenides 132d, 151e; Sophist 256b, 259a; Timaeus 77b; Laws IX 859e.

5 Phaedo 100d.

6 See Cornelio Fabro, *La nozione metafisica di partecipazione: secondo S. Tommaso d'Aquino*, 2nd ed. (Torino: Società Editrice Internazionale, 1950), 47.

7 David C. Schindler, 'What's the Difference? On the Metaphysics of Participation in a Christian Context', *The Saint Anselm Journal*, 3.1 (2005): 1–27; Fritz-Gregor Hermann, 'μετ-χειν, μεταλαμβ-νειν and the Problem of Participation in Plato's Ontology', *Philosophical Inquiry*, 25.3–4 (2003): 19–56, esp. 22–25.

understanding of participation convergent with the notion of taking a 'part in' (see Section 4).[8] The 'part of' terminology would seem to suggest that creatures have a 'part of', rather than a 'part in', God. With this there is the implication that the world is made from or out of God, with creation taking a part of the divine source. This divisibility conflicts with the definition of the conventional understanding of God, who possesses perfection, completely and totally. This brings us back to the sharing notion of participation mentioned above. If one participates in a team, one can play a position, fulfilling that role, without taking something from the team, whilst sharing in that team's reality. Indeed, rather than being reduced by playing one's position, the individual may be said to be increased by being more than what they would be without participating.[9] Therefore, participation is characterised by an activity of taking a 'part in' a relationship with God, not taking a 'part of' or 'part from' God.

The Language of Participating and Participated

In English, we most often encounter the verb 'participate' in an intransitive context as opposed to a transitive one. As such it takes an indirect object and not a direct object. For example, 'I participate in the rugby match', and never 'I participate the rugby match', or in the case of divine participation, 'the tree participates in God', and not 'God participates the tree'. The direct object constructions might ring strangely to our ears, yet they are not grammatically incorrect. In the case of the rugby match, if I (along with the other players involved) decided not to participate, then the match would not be participated, that is, it would not take place. This is even more so the case in the second example of divine participation. The tree participates in God, but if God does not participate the tree, then the tree would not exist, since God both creates and sustains the creature. Moreover, constructions such as 'the tree participates in God', which are not uncommon in English language descriptions of divine participation, are not as accurate as saying 'God participates the tree', since the former does not fully account for the absolutely asymmetrical relationship between God and creation. The indirect construction carried with it the potential for the statement to be interpreted to mean that the tree could continue to exist and not participate in God. Nevertheless, indirect statements concerning participation, divine or otherwise, are the idiomatic standard in contemporary

[8] See W. Norris Clarke, 'The Meaning of Participation in St. Thomas', in *Explorations in Metaphysics: Being, God, Persons* (Notre Dame: University of Notre Dame Press, 1994), 92–93.

[9] Andrew Davison, *Participation in God: A Study in Christian Doctrine and Metaphysics* (Cambridge: Cambridge University Press, 2019), 135–37.

English. In this examination both constructions are used, with the direct construction often being used for emphasis.

Participation's History

The concepts and the figures covered in this text offer an overview of divine participation. However, taken together they do not provide a history of participatory metaphysics, a task that is beyond the scope of this text. The best text on the history of participation is *Teilhabe: ein Schlüsselwort der Vätertheologie* by Friderich Normann, which details the history of the concept from early Presocratic instances through to Pseudo-Dionysius.[10] An excellent English language summary by Jacob Sherman sets forth a helpful genealogy of participation identifying three major developments, each of which are touched upon in the thematic sections that make up this text.[11] In the first stage, beginning with Plato, the focus is upon the participation of individual particular creatures in their essences, the archetypal forms. Jewish, Christian, and Pagan middle Platonist thinkers then adapted this, locating the forms in the divine mind (see Sections 2 and 3). In a second stage, centred upon the medieval period, the concept of participation is ontologically developed, focusing upon the participation of being, that is existence itself, in creatures (see Section 4). Finally, in a third stage, associated first with the Renaissance and then the Romantic period, the focus shifts to the participation of both the individual and creation in the divine in the context of an increasingly disenchanted understanding of nature (see Section 5).

In its ascendancy, participatory metaphysics had remarkable explanatory power, offering a coherent and elegant explanation of the relationship between the creator and the created, universals and particulars. At the same time, the metaphysics of participation had always been connected to a wider debate, as old as philosophy itself, between what can be called realism and nominalism. Realism is so named because it understands the universals in which individuals participate to be real, objective, and archetypical, and to reside in the realm of the intelligible independent of human thought. Realism understands these universal ideas as constitutive of reality in the context of the asymmetrical participatory metaphysics described above. Alternatively, the nominalist position understands universals to exist in things alone, or in the mind of the knower. This latter position gained increasing ascendancy beginning in the

[10] Friedrich Normann, *Teilhabe: ein Schlüsselwort der Vätertheologie* (Münster: Aschendorff, 1978).

[11] Jacob H. Sherman, 'A Genealogy of Participation', in *The Participatory Turn: Spirituality, Mysticism, Religious Studies*, ed. Jorge N. Ferrer and Jacob H. Sherman (Albany: State University of New York Press, 2008), 81–112.

late medieval period, particularly in the work of thinkers such as Scotus and Ockham. Though the precise role of the rise of nominalism in the decline of participatory metaphysics remains a matter of debate, by the advent of modernity, Cartesianism and Kantianism were dominant philosophical frameworks for conceptualising the world. Both understood the natural world to be autonomous from what came to be called the supernatural, establishing a framework of imminent naturalism that would be key to the development of the modern natural sciences.[12]

The rise of nominalism stressed a voluntarist understanding of the divine will, wherein all individuals are the product of divine sovereignty, as opposed to conforming to divinely determined universals. The intention in this context was to maintain God's absolute freedom in relation to creation, yet at the same time, it also had the effect of desacralizing creation through the withdrawal of the participatory relationship. This thinking in turn deeply influenced the Protestant Reformation and particularly Luther's denunciation of the presence of metaphysics in theology in favour of what has been called a biblical theology. In the late 19th and early 20th centuries, some elements of Protestant theology continued to advance a distrust of what it saw as Greek metaphysical influences upon the development of early Christianity. These Hellenistic accretions were understood by Adolf von Harnack as concealing what he considered to be the unphilosophical Hebrew religion upon which Christianity was founded, blurring the distinction between God and creatures, and obscuring Christian kerygma.[13] In a similar vein, there is a strong rejection of the tradition of natural theology in some aspects of the modern theological tradition, particularly as expressed by thinkers such as Karl Barth, for whom knowledge of God cannot

[12] For further analysis of this development, see Michael Allen Gillespie, *Nihilism before Nietzsche* (Chicago: University of Chicago Press, 1995); Catherine Pickstock, *After Writing: On the Liturgical Consummation of Philosophy* (Oxford: Blackwell, 1997); J. B. Schneewind, *The Invention of Autonomy: A History of Modern Moral Philosophy* (Cambridge: Cambridge University Press, 1998); Olivier Boulnois, *Être et représentation: une généalogie de la métaphysique moderne à l'époque de Duns Scot (XIIIe–XIVe siècle)* (Paris: Presses Universitaires de France, 1999); Richard Popkin, *The History of Scepticism: From Savonarola to Bayle* (Oxford: Oxford University Press, 2003); Jonathan I. Israel, *Radical Enlightenment: Philosophy and the Making of Modernity 1650–1750* (Oxford: Oxford University Press, 2001); Tad M. Schmaltz, *Radical Cartesianism: The French Reception of Descartes* (Cambridge: Cambridge University Press, 2002); Ludger Honnefelder, *Scientia Transcendens; Johannes Duns Scotus* (Munich: C. H. Beck, 2005); *Woher kommen wir? Ursprünge der Moderne im Denken des Mittelalters* (Berlin: Berlin University Press, 2008); Jan Aertsen, *Medieval Philosophy as Transcendental Thought: From Philip the Chancellor (ca. 1225) to Francisco Suarez* (Leiden: Brill, 2012); Alexander J. B. Hampton, *Romanticism and the Re-invention of Modern Religion: The Reconciliation of German Idealism and Platonic Realism* (Cambridge: Cambridge University Press, 2019).

[13] Adolf Harnack, *History of Dogma*, trans. Neil Buchanan, 7 vols. (London: Williams and Norgate, 1897) see esp. I, 46–47.

be ascertained outside of the domain of revelation.[14] Whilst this study does not proport to be a defence of participatory metaphysics, the sections that make up this text attempt to go some way to addressing some of these concerns, not least by considering some of the biblical sources of participatory thought, as well as its fundamental role in the history of Christianity's conceptualisation of itself, something attested to in Paul's Epistle to the Romans: 'Ever since the creation of the world his eternal power and divine nature, invisible though they are, have been understood and seen through the things he has made'.[15]

Many of these developments against participatory metaphysics fit within a progress narrative, or even a narrative of secularisation. Yet modernity does not lose participation so much as it transposes or transforms it in the increasingly complex context of modernity. Philosophers and theologians have continued to return to the idea, using it as an imaginative fulcrum for developing critiques of modernity, articulating transcendence-affirming forms of ecumenical and interreligious dialogue, and innovating new ways to reconceptualise nature in more sustainable and environmentally conscious non-anthropocentric contexts.[16] At the same time, an increasing number of academic monographs have examined participation in the thought of a range of figures from early Christianity through to modern Protestantism.[17] By far the most important of these has been *Participation in God*, by Andrew Davison. All of this points towards a return to the participatory tradition in the contemporary intellectual context.

---

[14] E.g. Karl Barth, *Nein!* (Munich: Kaiser, 1934).

[15] Romans 1:20. All Bible quotations are from the New Revised Standard Version.

[16] E.g. Sean McGrath, *Thinking Nature: An Essay in Negative Ecology* (Edinburgh: Edinburgh University Press, 2019); Alexander J. B. Hampton, 'Platonism, Nature and Environmental Crisis', in *Christian Platonism: A History*, ed. Alexander J. B. Hampton and John Kenney (Cambridge: Cambridge University Press, 2021), 381–407; 'Nature and Aesthetics: Methexis, Mimēsis and Poiēsis', in *Cambridge Companion to Christianity and the Environment*, ed. Alexander J. B. Hampton and Douglas Hedley (Cambridge: Cambridge University Press, 2022), 263–85; Michael Northcott, *God and Gaia: Science, Religion and Ethics on a Living Planet* (Abingdon: Routledge, 2023).

[17] See Melchisedec Törönen, *Union and Distinction in the Thought of St Maximus the Confessor* (Oxford: Oxford University Press, 2007); Todd J. Billings, *Calvin, Participation, and the Gift: The Activity of Believers in Union with Christ* (Oxford: Oxford University Press, 2007); Torstein Tollefsen, *The Christocentric Cosmology of St Maximus the Confessor* (Oxford: Oxford University Press, 2008); Olli-Pekk Vainio, *Justification and Participation in Christ: The Development of the Lutheran Doctrine of Justification from Luther to the Formula of Concord (1580)* (Leiden: Brill, 2008); S. T. Kimbrough, *Partakers of the Life Divine: Participation in the Divine Nature in the Writings of Charles Wesley* (Eugene: Cascade, 2016); Paul Anthony Dominiak, *Richard Hooker: The Architecture of Participation* (London: T&T Clark, 2019); Hampton, *Romanticism and the Re-invention of Modern Religion*; Yonghua Ge, *The Many and the One: Creation as Participation in Augustine and Aquinas* (Lanham: Lexington Books, 2021); Silvianne Aspray, *Metaphysics in the Reformation: The Case of Peter Martyr Vermigli* (Oxford: Oxford University Press, 2021).

2 Creation, the Divine Ideas, and the Origins of Participation

Creation is where participation occurs, making it an ideal theme with which to commence the contextual enquiry of this text. There is no participation without creation, and there is no creation without participation. Everything comes to creatures by participation, beginning with their very being and continuing with their attributes and end (or telos). We can understand creation as the movement from God as creator to creatures as the created, or to put it in the language of a classical formulation, as the way by which the One produces the many. Alternatively, we can conceptualise participation as the movement from creatures towards God, and as the way the many relate back to and desire the One which is their source. In this manner the consideration of creation is both cosmological in terms of a search for origins, and ontological in the sense of discerning the general rules that govern that creation. We can observe participatory thought at work in the Bible, and in the thought of early Jewish and Christian thinkers, including Philo of Alexandria (c. 20 BC–c. AD 40) and Augustine of Hippo (AD 354–430), both of whom are considered here. Their thought develops in a cultural context that is deeply influenced by Hellenistic philosophy, and particularly the writings of Plato (427 BC–346 BC) and his followers.[18] Indeed, it is in the thought of Plato that the concept of participation received its first philosophical articulation, that is, in Plato's writing it was first presented in a metaphysical and reasoned account, rather than the contextual manifestations already present in scripture. In the complex intellectual environment of overlapping influences and traditions from which Christianity emerged, the Christian concept of the metaphysics of participation would begin to develop. Though this process remains the topic of enduring academic speculation, for the sake of this study, the development of the Christian conceptualisation of the divine ideas, and the role it plays in the development of the doctrine of creation, provides the means to trace the emergence of the participatory tradition in Latin Christianity.[19]

The Divine Ideas

The notion of the divine ideas has been key in conceptualising the participatory relationship between God and creation. As one of the most significant

[18] John Peter Kenney, *Mystical Monotheism: A Study in Ancient Platonic Theology* (Hanover: Brown University Press, 1991); E. R. Dodds, *Pagan and Christian in an Age of Anxiety: Some Aspects of Religious Experience from Marcus Aurelius to Constantine* (Cambridge: Cambridge University Press, 1968); Mark Edwards, *Culture and Philosophy in the Age of Plotinus* (London: Duckworth, 2006); George Karamanolis, *The Philosophy of the Early Church* (New York: Abingdon, 2021).

[19] Mark Clavier, *Eloquent Wisdom: Rhetoric, Cosmology and Delight in the Theology of Augustine of Hippo* (Belgium: Brepols, 2014), 113.

notions in Christian intellectual history, it has been a locus for the employment and development of the concept of participation.[20] The divine ideas are best understood as the archetypes in God's mind in which creation participates. These archetypes make an account of God's rationality possible. They provide a framework whereby human inquiry can discern a logic that precedes creation, which is purposeful and intelligible, which has a process and an end, and which consequently can be understood, at least in part, by human rationality. The divine ideas have largely been understood in an analogical context, that is, as an imperfect way for human minds to creatively approximate the workings of a God who is beyond intellectual circumscription. The divine ideas can be contrasted to human ideas which are limited, both in their scope and definition, and by the capacity of the minds that think them. Even in the best circumstances, where human minds exceed their capacities, their ideas remain limited by time and space. Consequently, even the divine ideas that human minds think are arrived at evolve through contemplation and experience in the historical and situational context in which they are encountered.

Divine ideas are only fully released in the mind of God, but never fully and perfectly participated in creatures, whether in the mind of the individual, or in a particular creature. It is impossible for any particular creature to either cognitively or physically possess the transcendent totality of, for example, the beautiful. Instead, through participation, writes Pseudo-Dionysius (5th–6th c.), an important figure in the divine ideas tradition, God 'deals out the immeasurable and infinite in limited measure'.[21] Consequently, whilst human ideas bear a similarity to these divine ideas, they are not the same. God's ideas are not the product of a process of discovery, conjecture, and experimentation, as they are with humans, nor do they slowly unfold, rather, they precede any instantiation of themselves. For example, in Genesis, when God says, '"Let there be light"; and there was light', the idea precedes the instantiation.[22] Divine ideas are different in that they are perfect, fully realised, and unchanging, neither coming to be nor passing away. These divine ideas therefore are immutable, universal, and perfect, transcending

[20] See also Kenney, *Mystical Monotheism*, 15–31; John Dillon and Daniel J. Tolan, 'Ideas as Thoughts of God', in *Christian Platonism: A History*, ed. Alexander J. B. Hampton and John Peter Kenney (Cambridge: Cambridge University Press, 2021), 34–52; Alexander J. B. Hampton, 'God's Ideas', in *T&T Clark Encyclopedia of Christian Theology*, ed. Jana Bennett, Stephen Cone, and Jason Fout (New York: Bloomsbury), in press.

[21] Pseudo Dionysius, 'Divine Names', in *Pseudo-Dionysius: Complete Works*, trans. Colm Luibheid (New York: Paulist Press, 1987), 588A.

[22] Gen 1:3; For the non-temporal nature of the statement see Jonathan Yovel, 'The Creation of Language and Language without Time: Metaphysics and Metapragmatics in Genesis 1', *Biblical Interpretation*, 20.3 (2012): 205–25.

any particular creaturely instantiation. As we will come to see in the course of this examination, creatures participate in divine ideas, and without divine ideas, there are no creatures.

The Hebrew Bible

There is no technical articulation of the process of participation or the metaphysics of the divine ideas in the Bible. Nevertheless, that they are not conceptually or technically articulated does not mean that they are extrinsic to the text, and indeed to demand such an articulation would be anachronistic. Instead, the reader encounters them, embodied and contextual, in the theological and philosophical idiom of their age, the biblical text itself.[23] As the following section focuses upon the New Testament, and particularly the incarnation, here we turn our attention to the Hebrew Bible. What we find in it is a presupposition that the world participates in a divine plan. For example, when God creates vegetation in the Genesis creation story there comes to be a vast variety that corresponds to their kind: 'Then God said, "Let the earth put forth vegetation: plants yielding seed, and fruit trees of every kind on earth that bear fruit with the seed in it." And it was so. The earth brought forth vegetation: plants yielding seed of every kind, and trees of every kind bearing fruit with the seed in it. And God saw that it was good'.[24] The same pattern follows for the creation of animals.[25] According to the Book of Proverbs, Wisdom, which was created by God at the beginning of the world, worked beside God as a 'master worker', and continues to order the world, such that those who seek Wisdom in creation find happiness, knowledge and prosperity by attuning themselves to God's creation.[26] Similarly, the Book of Wisdom describes how God ordered 'all things by measure, and number, and weight', concepts contained in the divine ideas.[27] Also, in the Hebrew Bible we find claim that, as part of creation, humans participate in divine action through their own actions: 'all that we have done, you have done for us'.[28] Importantly, this means that humans are integrally part of creation, intimately involved in the realisation of the divine ideas. Human creativity participates in divine creativity and is not somehow separate from creation or God. Overall, what the Bible communicates is that there is no part of creation that is separate from, or not

[23] Mark Glouberman, *Persons and Other Things: Exploring the Philosophy of the Hebrew Bible* (Toronto: University of Toronto Press, 2021); Claude Tresmontant and Ronald Koshoshek, 'Biblical Metaphysics', *Cross Currents*, 10.3 (1960): 229–50, esp. 229–31; Claude Tresmontant, *Études de métaphysique biblique* (Paris: Gabalda, 1955).

[24] (Gen. 1.11–12). [25] (Gen. 20–1; 24–5). [26] Prov. 8.30; 8.22. [27] Wis 11.20.

[28] (Is. 26.12).

participating in, God's ideas. This is eloquently and succinctly expressed in Isaiah:

> I am the Lord, and there is no other;
> besides me there is no god.
> I arm you, though you do not know me,
> so that they may know, from the rising of the sun
> and from the west, that there is no one besides me;
> I am the Lord, and there is no other.
> I form light and create darkness,
> I make weal and create woe;
> I the Lord do all these things.[29]

Here, everything that falls under the sweep of the sun's motion across the heavens participates in God. All that seems good, and even all that seems bad from the human perspective, and the very light by which one encounters both, participate in God.

Plato & Philo

A similar way of thinking about the relationship between the divine and the created world was also present in pagan Greek thought. Presocratic philosophers such as Thales (5th–6th c. BC) asserted that 'all things are full of Gods', and Heraclitus (6th c. BC) similarly postulated that 'all things are filled with souls and divinities'.[30] This way of thinking came to be formalised in the philosophy of Plato, for whom participation (methexis) was the means to address how a singular concept could be predicated of multiple particular things.[31] According to Plato, all appearances are said to be 'derived' from the ideas (or forms) which are their 'ground'.[32] For example, in the *Republic*, we read 'beauty itself and good itself and all the things that we thereby set down as many, reversing ourselves, we set down according to a single form of each, believing that there is but one, and call it "the being" of each'.[33] Plato's reasoning is that wherever there is a mini there must be a one, wherever there is a multiplicity of individuals that share a common attribute there must be a supreme and perfect 'being' of that attribute, its idea.

The ideas are apprehended through a combination of perception and anamnesis (i.e., rational intuition drawn from memory). Plato puts forward this theory, particularly in the *Meno* and *Phaedo* dialogues, which elaborate

[29] Isaiah 45.5–7.

[30] Thales, DK 11A22 (Aristotle, *De Anima* 411a9); Diogenes Laertius, *Lives of the Eminent Philosophers*, trans. R. D. Hicks, Loeb Classical Library (Cambridge, MA: Harvard University Press, 1925), 9.7.

[31] Eg. *Rep.* X 596, a6-7. [32] *Phaedo* 100d-101a. [33] Rep. 507b.

a position wherein humans have a knowledge of the forms which arise in empirical experience but also exceed it, revealing the eternal soul's prenatal experience of the forms in themselves.[34] The process of recollection, which provokes a desire to recall what the soul once fully knew, is Plato's explanation for the basic human desire to know, and the shared love of wisdom which becomes philosophy. In Plato's philosophy, knowledge is participatory in the sense that all things, both the objects we experience and the mind that thinks them, participate in meaning that exists beyond them in the ideas. These ideas are immutable, eternal, divine, and incorporeal, but they are not the ideas in the mind of a creator God.[35] The role of the ideas is elaborated in a cosmological context in the cosmogony of the *Timaeus*, which explains that the structure given to the cosmos is the product of the good intent of God, who through the figure of the Craftsman (Demiurge), using the intelligible ideas as a model, shaped pre-existent chaos into as excellent a creation as possible through participation in these ideas.[36] From this, one can see that in Plato's cosmogony the universe was made of pre-existent matter, something which Christianity would come to reject in favor of the view of creation out of nothing (creatio ex nihilo).[37] Plato's thought, shaped as it was in the context of the Pythagorean and Parmenidean philosophies that preceded him, identified the infinite with unintelligibility and chaos, and hence conceived of it negatively. Alternatively, finitude, as we can see reflected in the activity of the demiurge, provided interlegibility and proportion through the ideas. As a result, Plato's philosophy does not have the notion that would later characterise Christian thought, wherein creation receives in a limited way what is unlimited in God.

An essential step towards the Christian concept of the divide ideas occurred with Philo with whom we can observe the conceptualisation of the Platonic ideas as forming the contents of the divine intellect. This was probably first expressed in the thought of the middle Platonist Antiochus (c. 125 BC–c. 68 BC).[38] However, it was the influential figure of Philo of Alexandria who brought together the Greek and Hebrew traditions in his *On the Account of the World's Creation Given by Moses* (*De opificio mundi*).[39] Plato's cosmogony would have philosophically appealed to Philo and his Alexandrian contemporaries because of the similarity between the Demiurge and the creator God in Genesis. Many pagan philosophers argued that the cosmos was characterised by intelligibility and goodness, yet Plato alone suggested that these features were externally imposed upon it. Additionally, the *Timaeus* made the argument that creation itself was good and

[34] *Phd* 77a-c, 79b-e, 91e-92b Meno, 81b-e. [35] *Phd* 78d, 79d, 80a-b.
[36] *Tim* 28a-b; 29e-30d. [37] E.g. Theophilus of Antioch, *Apologia ad Autolycum* II.4.
[38] Dillon & Tolan, 'Ideas as Thoughts of God', 27–41.
[39] David T. Runia, *Philo of Alexandria and the Timaeus of Plato* (Leiden: Brill, 1968).

beautiful; a claim which was in sympathy with the Hebrew Bible's account of the goodness of creation.[40]

In a passage that is plainly indebted to the *Timaeus*, Philo writes that 'when he [God] willed to create this visible world he first fully formed the intelligible world in order that he might have the use of a pattern wholly God-like and incorporeal in producing the material world'.[41] Philo then elegantly elaborates this through a metaphor wherein God is likened to a master planner commissioned with the building of a new city. This architect first mentally devises the parts of the city, which are then realised in physical form.[42] Just as all of the built city participates in the plan of the architect, all of creation participates in the divine ideas which God conceives before the creation itself. Philo's location of Plato's ideas in the mind of the creator God of Genesis would have a significant influence on the development of the Christian metaphysics of participation. The divine ideas furnished the nascent religion with a participatory framework for conceptualising the God–creation relationship which subsequent thinkers adapted and modified according to the needs of the Christian tradition, as we can see when turning to the thought of Augustine of Hippo.

Augustine

Augustine is one of the most influential figures in Western Christian theology, and an important transitional figure writing at the close of antiquity on the cusp of the early mediaeval period. Augustine played an important role in determining the relationship between Christianity and Platonism, the latter of which was highly influential upon shaping his faith.[43] Comparing the school of Hellenic philosophy to Christianity, Augustine wrote that 'there are none who come nearer to us than the Platonists'.[44] Despite this, Augustine also plays an important role in marking out the distinctions that would come to separate Christian Platonism from that of its pagan counterpart.[45] Central to this process

[40] George Karamanolis, 'Creation in Early Christianity', in *The Routledge Handbook of Early Christian Philosophy*, ed. Mark Edwards (London: Rutledge, 2020), 56.

[41] Philo of Alexandria, 'On the Account of the World's Creation Given by Moses', in *Philo Volume I*, trans. G. H. Whitaker, Loeb Classical Library (Cambridge, MA: Harvard University Press, 1929), 4.16; Cf. Tim. 28ab, 29e, 30d, 48e.

[42] *Opif.* 4.17–18.

[43] Brian Dobell, *Augustine's Intellectual Conversion: The Journey from Platonism to Christianity* (Cambridge: Cambridge University Press, 2009); John Peter Kenney, *The Mysticism of St Augustine: Rereading the Confessions* (London: Rutledge, 2005).

[44] Augustine, *City of God*, trans. Henry Bettenson, Penguin Classics (London: Penguin Books, 1972), 8.5.

[45] John Peter Kenney, '"None Come Closer to Us than These": Augustine and the Platonists', *Religions*, 7.9 (2016): 114; John Peter Kenney, 'Platonism and Christianity in Late Antiquity', in *Christian Platonism: A History*, ed. Alexander J. B. Hampton and John Peter Kenney (Cambridge: Cambridge University Press), 177–79.

would be his development of a distinctly Christian formulation of participatory metaphysics. He would do this in the context of his consideration of creation, a central theme throughout his theology, revising the notion of the divine ideas by reading them in the context of the doctrine of creatio ex nihilo and the consequent goodness of creation that necessarily arises from it.[46]

For Augustine, the notion of the divine ideas is the basis for understanding the relationship between God and creation, which in turn places participation at the centre of his theology.[47] In an early text, Augustine offers this definition of the ideas:

> ideas are the principle forms or the fixed and unchangeable reasons of things that have themselves not been formed and consequently are eternal, always constituted in the same way and contained in the divine intelligence. And although these neither come into existence nor perish, nonetheless everything that *can* come into existence and perish and everything that *does* come into existence and perish is said to be formed in accordance with them.[48]

In passages such as this, we can observe how the divine ideas become the heuristic matrix wherein participation functions as the means to conceptualise one's relationship to, understanding of, and response to God. For instance, the same text opens with the statement that *Omne verum a veritate verum est* ('Everything that is true is true by reason of the truth'). Here 'verum' has its reality because it participates in 'veritas'.[49] Alternatively, 'veritas', the divine idea, is fully realised and unchanging, whilst 'verum' requires a participatory relationship for its very existence. As we can see, in the context of Plato and Philo, the model for Augustine is decidedly Platonic, with ideas such as beauty, goodness, and truth, being participated in the particular creatures in which they are instantiated by the divine ideas.[50] Creatures remain mutable because their participation in these ideas is always partial, whilst at the same time they are dependent upon the reality of the divine ideas for their existence as such.

Augustine considers the notion of the divine ideas in the context of creation in the twelfth book of the *Confessions*. There, he offers an interpretation of the initial lines of Genesis concerning God's creation of heaven and earth. He

[46] Augustine considered creation throughout his intellectual career in *On Genesis against the Manichees* (388/9); *On the Literal Meaning of Genesis, Unfinished*: (393); *Confessions* XI–XII (397–400); *The Literal Meaning of Genesis* (404–20); *City of God* XI–XII.

[47] David V. Meconi, 'St. Augustine's Early Theory of Participation', *Augustinian Studies*, 27 (1996): 83; Claudio Moreschini, 'Neoplatonismo e cristianesimo: 'Partecipare d Dio' secondo Boezio e Agostino', in *Sicilia e Italia suburbicaria tra IV e VIII secolo*, ed. Salvatore Pricoco, et al. (Soveria Mannelli: Rubbettino Editore, 1991), 283–95.

[48] Augustine, 'Miscellany of Eighty-Three Questions', in *Responses to Miscellaneous Questions*, trans. Boniface Ramsey, The Works of Saint Augustine: A Translation for the 21st Century (Hyde Park: New City Press, 2008),46.2, Italics original.

[49] *Div. Qu.* 1.1. [50] E.g. see *Div. Qu.* 23.

maintains that these are not to be understood literally as the sky and the land, but as the establishment of two extreme and abstract versions of created reality: formless matter and the heaven of heavens.[51] The former participates in something akin to pure potentiality, and is, according to Augustine, 'almost nothing'.[52] The latter heaven of heavens is an intelligible creature that differs in kind from the firmament, or heavens, which exist in relation to the earth and sea:[53]

> 'heaven' means the 'heaven of heaven', the intellectual, non-physical heaven where the intelligence's knowing is a matter of simultaneity – not in part, not in an enigma, not through a mirror, but complete, in total openness, 'face to face' (I Cor. 13: 12). This knowing is not of one thing at one moment and of another thing at another moment, but is concurrent without any temporal successiveness.[54]

Here, the heaven of heavens is immutable, and timeless, but it is not coeternal with God since it is created by God at the very inception of creation. At the same time, it is very much unlike the other creatures that would follow it. Its special nature is to exist in direct and uninterrupted communion with God. Augustine writes that 'not even that created realm the "heaven of heavens", is co-eternal with you. In an unfailing purity it satiates its thirst in you. It never at any point betrays its mutability. You are always present to it, and it concentrates all its affection on you. It has no future to expect. It suffers no variation and experiences no distending in the successiveness of time'.[55] The heaven of heavens contains the divine ideas in their full and unchanging realisation. They are the intelligible reality in which all creatures participate in a less than full and perfect way. Here, according to Augustine's reasoning, the ideas are preserved, and not by necessity, but by divine love. This has the benefit of ensuring that the divine ideas, whilst themselves participating in God's nature, are not themselves equal to God. Unlike Plato, there is no independent model to which God looks when fashioning creation as a divine artisan. Instead, the dependent ideas in the heaven of heavens are the models. This formulation also has the benefit of outlining the ontological distinction between God and creation. It is the nature of all creatures to participate in the divine ideas. However, God's eternal nature as the creator of these ideas remains transcendent of creation, avoiding any

---

51 Augustine, *Confessions*, XII.2–6.

52 *Conf.* XII.8; Rowan Williams, 'Creation', in *Augustine through the Ages*, ed. Allan D. Fitzgerald (Grand Rapids: William B. Eerdmans, 1999), 252.

53 *Conf.* XII.8–9.

54 *Conf.* XII.13.16, trans. Henry Chadwick (Oxford: Oxford University Press, 2008). Cf. Phaedrus 247c-e.

55 *Conf.* XII.11.12.

pantheistic equation of God and creation, whilst simultaneously allowing God to be imminently present throughout creation, through the participatory role of the Ideas.

What begins to distinguish Augustine's position from that of Plato and Philo, however, is not so much the concept of the heaven of heavens but his consideration of the Platonic heritage in the context of the doctrine of creatio ex nihilo. In Plato's cosmogony, as with some early Christian thinkers as well, the universe was made of pre-existent matter.[56] However, in time, as Christian thought developed, this came to be rejected, especially in the context of Christian-Gnostic debates.[57] Whether the doctrine of creation ex nihilo has singularly biblical origins, or emerged out of biblical considerations that responded to Greek philosophy remains a matter of debate. However, its development results in a Christian position that explicitly rejected one of the central notions of Hellenistic philosophy, namely the principle that ex nihilo nihil fit (out of nothing comes nothing).[58] As a doctrine, it became central to Christianity as is attested to in the opening claim the Nicene creed, which declares God to be the 'maker of all things, visible and invisible'. As Augustine's participatory view of creation shows, it becomes a means to stress the ontological division between God and creation, the intrinsic dependence of creation upon God, and the fundamental goodness of that creation.

Above all, the most important result of the consideration of participation in the context of creatio ex nihilo is the convertibility of being and goodness on the level of creative things. In contrast to the widely held Greek position, including that of Platonic philosophy, that creation is made from pre-existent eternal matter, Augustine maintains that 'even if the world was made out of some unshaped, formless matter, this was itself made out of absolutely nothing'.[59] Moreover, since God is by nature good, humans must conclude that created existence is intrinsically good in itself, as the Genesis creation narrative attests. Creation is a gift from God who is by nature supremely good.

In his consideration of good and evil in the *Enchiridion*, Augustine sets out how creation shares in the goodness of God, but that the goodness of creatures

---

[56] Justin, *Apologia*, 1.59; Clement of Alexandria, *Stromata*, V.14.

[57] E.g. Theophilus of Antioch, *Apologia ad Autolycum*, II.4.

[58] Ernan McMullin, 'Creation Ex Nihilo: Early History', in *Creation and the God of Abraham*, ed. David B. Burrell, et al. (Cambridge: Cambridge University Press, 2010), 11–23; Frances Young, '"CreatioEx Nihilo": A Context for the Emergence of the Christian Doctrine of Creation', *Scottish Journal of Theology*, 44.2 (1991): 139–51; Janet M. Soskice, 'Creatio Ex Nihilo: Jewish and Christian Foundations', in *Creation and the God of Abraham*, ed. David B. Burrell, et al. (Cambridge: Cambridge University Press, 2010), 30–31.

[59] Agustine, 'True Religion', in *On Christian Belief*, ed. Boniface Ramsey, trans. Edmund Hill, The Works of Saint Augustine: A Translation for the 21st Century (Hyde Park: New City Press, 2005), 8.36.

differs in degree from divine goodness.[60] He explains that 'all things are good, since the maker of all things is supremely good. But since they are not supremely and unchangeably good like their creator, in them goodness can be decreased and increased'.[61] Nevertheless, since all things are created by God through his goodness, existence by its very being must continue to be good. Augustine continues, 'for good to be decreased is evil, even though, however much it is decreased, some of it must remain for the thing to exist at all, if it does still exist'.[62] For Augustine, there is nothing that is truly absolutely evil. To exist is to participate in being, and being by its very nature is good. This is not to deny the existence of evil but rather, as Augustine writes, 'every being, even if it is corrupt, insofar as it is a being is good and insofar as it is corrupt is evil'.[63] Consequently, in the context of Augustine's participatory view of creation, evil may only exist as a parasitic deprivation of the good, lessening the reality of that from which it takes.

The view of creation as fundamentally good that arises out of creatio ex nihilo results in a specifically Christian version of participatory metaphysics for Augustine. Creation is not a lesser facsimile of an abstract intelligible idea, rather it is the creature coming to the idea. Ideas and creation are ontologically distinct, and consequently exist in a non-contrastive relation to one another. As a result, creaturely reality is not something that needs to be escaped in order to encounter the divine ideas as they truly are, which can be a tendency in both Platonic and Gnostic-influenced forms of Christian thought. Rather, creation is the very arena in which the divine ideas may be encountered for creatures. There is no other abstract alternative to creation. Creation cannot be conceived of negatively in terms of lack. Instead, the multiplicity that characterises creation discloses the oneness of God in a manner appropriate to the unique nature of each particular participating creature. In Augustine's participatory ontology, God is both transcendent, as the cause of all creation, and immanent, in a sustaining participatory relationship with it. This coincidence of transcendence and immanence also expresses the radically non-dualistic nature of creation. Though there undoubtedly remains a tendency to prioritise the transcendent over the immanent, and spirit over matter in Christian thought, the goodness of creation, which arises directly out of the consequences of creatio ex nihilo, resists the establishment of a world-denying contemptus mundi in the context considered here.

The participation of creation in the divine ideas, and the intrinsic goodness of that creation by having its source in God, provides an impetus to natural

---

[60] Augustine, 'Enchiridion', in *On Christian Belief*, ed. Boniface Ramsey, trans. Bruce Harbert, The Works of Saint Augustine: A Translation for the 21st Century (Hyde Park: New City Press, 2005), 3.9.

[61] *Ench*, 4.12. [62] *Ench*, 4.12. [63] *Ench*, 4.13.

theology alongside revelation for Augustine. Humans are called to respond to the participatory nature of creation, whose didactic quality, explains Augustine, is both redemptive and doxological:

> Take a look at the structure of the world, observe what has been made through the Word, and then you will have some idea of what the Word is like. Take a look at the two parts of the world, heaven and earth; who can find words to talk about the splendor of the heavens? Who can find words to talk about the fruitfulness of the earth? Who can fittingly praise the changing seasons?[64]

In the goodness of creation, in its enveloping vastness and its sublime proportions, the divine ideas are disclosed to human beings through participation. Creation therefore comes to be seen, in many aspects of the Christian tradition, as a place of divine revelation, a second book, alongside the Bible, where divinity makes itself known in created reality.

Creation as Revelation

This revelatory view of creation was not an invention that simply grew out of Greek influences in the development of Christian theology. It is something that finds expression in the Bible itself which commends it. The meaning and purpose of creation was something that could be read through its participatory nature. In an evocative passage from the book of Job we read: 'But ask the animals, and they will teach you; the birds of the air, and they will tell you; ask the plants of the earth, and they will teach you; and the fish of the sea will declare to you. Who among all these does not know that the hand of the Lord has done this?'[65] In the New Testament, Jesus uses a range of images such as the mustard seed, fish, grapes, lilies, water, vines, and sparrows, all to communicate the reality of the divine ideas for humans in the form of moral lessons. The reading of the book of nature is therefore a dialogical practice where humans read creation through a process that ideally leads to greater integration with its meaning and purpose as instituted by its creator.

The dual interpretation of both scripture and nature would develop into the two books tradition, where both the Bible and creation provide edification and a means of ascent for humans towards God.[66] The concept would come to be highly influential in the medieval period in the work of figures such as William of

64 Augustine, *Homilies on the Gospel of John 1–40*, trans. Edmund Hill, The Works of Saint Augustine: A Translation for the 21st Century (Hyde Park: New City Press, 2009), 1.9.

65 Job 12:7–9.

66 Peter Harrison, *The Bible, Protestantism, and the Rise of Natural Science* (Cambridge: Cambridge University Press, 1998), 45–56; Jacob Holsinger Sherman, 'The Book of Nature',

Conches (c. 1090–1154), Alain de Lille (c. 1128–1202), Robert Grosseteste (1175–1254), and Bonaventure (1221–1274), who writes in his *Journey of the Mind to God* that 'We may behold God in the mirror of visible creation, not only by considering creatures as vestiges of God, but also by seeing Him in them; for He is present in them by His essence, His power, and His presence'.[67] In this participatory context, God is not merely present in nature as a designer, but is truly present in it, something we will come to see in greater detail in the thought of Aquinas in the fourth section. It is because of participation that Bonaventure claims 'we ought to be led to the contemplation of God in every creature that enters our mind through the bodily senses'.[68] This creates a markedly different relationship between human beings and nature than the one that adheres in a modern context, where the meaning and purpose of nature has traditionally resided in the human mind alone, sometimes with deleterious environmental consequences.[69]

The divine ideas provided a way to address two fundamental questions that were of central concern to Christianity, particularly in the period of its early development. First, they provided a way to conceptualise the cosmological question of how creation comes into being. At the same time, they addressed the further ontological question concerning the general structure of creation, and how it ought to be understood. As such, the divine ideas influenced the development of the Christian metaphysics of participation. As we have seen, particularly in the thought of Augustine, considered in the context of the creatio ex nihilo, they helped to furnish a view of creation as a place of divine encounter. This was a unique development, marking off Christian participation from those philosophical forms which preceded it, especially through the non-contrastive nature of the creator–creation relationship that emerged from the participatory metaphysics of creation.

3 Being and Becoming in God through Incarnation and Salvation

The previous section took up cosmological and ontological questions concerning the coming to be of creation and the principles that govern it. With

in *The Cambridge Companion to Christianity and the Environment*, ed. Alexander J. B. Hampton and Douglas Hedley (Cambridge: Cambridge University Press, 2022), 96–113.

67 Bonaventure, *The Journey of the Mind to God*, trans. Philotheus Boehner (Indianapolis: Hackett, 1993), 2.1.

68 *Itin.*, 2.1.

69 See Alexander J. B. Hampton, 'Platonism, Nature and Environmental Crisis', in *Christian Platonism: A History*, ed. Alexander J. B. Hampton and John Peter Kenney (Cambridge: Cambridge University Press, 2021), 381–407; Alexander J. B. Hampton, 'Nature and Aesthetics: Methexis, Mimēsis and Poiēsis', in *The Cambridge Companion to Christianity and the Environment*, ed. Alexander J. B. Hampton and Douglas Hedley (Cambridge: Cambridge University Press, 2022), 263–85.

these broad topics addressed we can turn to the anthropological question of the place of humans within this participatory cosmos. As already noted (Section 1), tension can arise in the thought of human beings concerning their creaturely being and the knowledge and proximity to God that they desire. This tension can lead to the devaluation of creaturely being, and especially the human body, which can come to be seen as a barrier or hindrance. For Irenaeus of Lyon (c. 130–202), whose thought this section focuses upon, this tension arises out of a misunderstanding of the place of humans within the participatory cosmos. He argues that creaturely being is essential for participation, something which makes creation in general, and bodily human existence in particular, good. For Irenaeus, humans have not only a general participatory relationship with God as their creator and sustainer, but they also have a particular relationship with God whose incarnation makes possible their salvation. With the assistance of the thought of Hans Urs von Balthasar (1905–1988), this section will explore how the participatory relationship that human beings have with God in the Christian context is much more dynamic than a one-directional creator–creature relationship. It is also characterised by the drama of becoming towards God, a drama which unfolds in the story of God's incarnation and participation in the life of humanity, and the response of each individual human being to the salvation which the incarnation makes available to them. In this section, the participatory creation described in the previous section becomes the stage upon which the divine–human encounter unfolds, where individuals find themselves to be both audience members and participants.

Irenaeus of Lyons

Irenaeus was born in Greek speaking Asia Minor, probably in Smyrna (present day Izmir, Turkey), and rose to become the Bishop of Lugdunum (Lyons). He is best known for his substantive five-book work *On the Detection and Overthrow of the So-Named Gnosis*, usually referred to by the translation of its Latin title *Against Heresies* (*Adversus Haereses*), written around the year 180. It was originally written in Greek but survives in its entirety only in Latin translation. The work itself is not a systematic theology, so much as it is the contextual response of his orthodox Christianity to the Gnostic and Marcionite movements active within the religious debates of his day, and which he understood as falsifying and distorting the Christian message. At this time, scarcely a century old, the orthodoxy Irenaeus sought to defend should not yet be conflated with a majority position. Indeed, he came to Lyon after the martyrdom of his predecessor (Pothinos, d.177) and the persecution of the Christian community there.

The particularity of the debates he engaged in with heretical movements are not of central concern here. However, two broad positions which Irenaeus sought to refute would structure a theological response in which he would develop a highly participatory theology deeply concerned with the place of humans in creation, and how this place is shaped by the incarnation and salvation. First, Irenaeus opposed the Gnostic claim that salvation arose from the possession of special knowledge, divine gnosis. Second, he opposed a Gnostic claim, particularly manifest in the Marcionite movement, that the material world was the creation of a lesser God, the Old Testament God, who was distinct from the God revealed in the New Testament. Both of these positions led to a negative valuation of creation in general and of embodied human beings in particular. The consequence of this negative valuation was to render knowledge of God, and particularly that of salvation, into something that could be achieved only through an escape from creaturely reality. For Irenaeus, this Gnostic view of creation threatened the very life of human beings by conceptualising creaturely being and divine transcendence as a competition between the spiritual and the physical. Irenaeus argued that this view threatened a kind of 'homicide' (in his words) because it so degraded the importance of the creaturely reality of humans.[70] Contrastingly, Irenaeus defended the orthodox positions of the centrality of faith, the goodness of creation, and the oneness of God.

Being and Becoming

Irenaeus structures his theological reasoning in a way that makes use of the central Platonic distinction between being and becoming, which is found throughout the works of Plato and the later developers of the Platonic tradition. Though there were naturally many points at which Irenaeus' Christianity was at odds with Plato's philosophy, he expresses an admiration for him above that of his heretical opponents, particularly because of Plato's defence of the goodness of creation. In comparison to the Gnostic writers, Irenaeus favourably comments that 'Plato is shown to be more religious than these men . . . . He sets down God's goodness as the beginning and cause of the creation of the world'.[71] The essential goodness of creation was a distinguishing position between Christianity, with its notion of divine

[70] *Adv. Haer.* III.16.8; Julie Canlis, 'Being Made Human: The Significance of Creation for Irenaeus's Doctrine of Participation', *Scottish Journal of Theology*, 58.4 (2005): 434–54.

[71] *Adv. Haer.* III.25.5 All quotations of *Adversus Haereses* are from *St. Irenaeus of Lyons: Against the Heresies*, trans. Dominic J. Unger, et al., Ancient Christian Writers (Mahwah: Paulist Press,

incarnation as central to salvation, and its Gnostic opposite which conceptualised creation as a barrier to salvation and God. Plato's concept of being and becoming is most explicitly articulated in the *Timaeus*, the highly influential cosmogony encountered in the previous section. In that dialogue, Plato offers the following formulation through the character of Timaeus: What is that which always is and has no becoming, and what is that which becomes but never is? The former is grasped by understanding, which involves a reasoned account. It is unchanging. The latter is grasped by opinion, which involves unreasoning sense perception'.[72]

The being and becoming distinction is central to Plato and the subsequent Greek Platonic philosophical tradition to which Irenaeus, along with his fellow early Greek Christian thinkers, were exposed.[73]

As we have already seen, Plato's philosophical system offered a creation narrative in which a creator God, the demiurge, looks upon intelligible ideas as the model for the cosmos. These intelligible ideas have the nature of unchanging being, and the created cosmos exists in a relationship of becoming in relation to them. We also observed how this was adapted into the divine ideas tradition, establishing a framework for an asymmetrical participatory relationship between the ideas and their instantiation in any creatures that participate in them. In turning to Irenaeus, what we find is an exploration of this participatory relation that is specifically focused upon God and humans:

> God differs from man in this, that God makes, but man is made. And he who makes is always the same, but he who is made must receive a beginning and a middle, a growing and maturing. God, again, gives benefits; Man receives benefits. God is perfect in every respect, being equal and similar to himself, since he is all light and all mind and all substance and the fount of all good. But man makes progress toward God and receives an increase. In fact, just as God is always the same, so man is found in God and always makes progress toward God. For neither does God ever cease bestowing gifts on man and enriching him, nor does man cease receiving gifts and being enriched by God.[74]

What we can observe moving here from Plato to Irenaeus with these passages is the Christianisation of the intrinsically participatory being and becoming relationship. Humans are made by God 'who is', and humans exist in

1992–2024) with reference to *Irénée de Lyon Contre les Hérésies: Édition Critique*, ed. Adelin Rousseau, et al., Sources Chrétiennes (Éditions du Cerf: Paris, 1952–82).

72 *Tim.* 27d-28a, Plato, *Complete Works*, ed. John M. Cooper, trans. Donald J. Zeyl (Indianapolis: Hackett, 1997).

73 Denis Minns, *Irenaeus: An Introduction* (London: T&T Clark, 2010), 83–91.

74 *Adv. Haer.* IV.11.2.

a process of becoming, with beginning, middle, and maturation. Apart from Plato, Irenaeus emphasises the personal and dynamic context of the relationship. God gives benefits and gifts, whilst humans receive them. Humans can make themselves open to this relationship, as willing participants in the metaphysics of participation, becoming, in Irenaeus' words, 'the receptacle of his goodness and the product of his glory'.[75] Alternatively, they may choose to turn from God, making themselves the receptacle of his judgment.[76] In either case, participation retains in a fuller or lesser form, though it is the chosen path of openness that constitutes the way to salvation according to Irenaeus.

The dynamism described here is extended in Irenaeus' language of 'progress towards God', whose perfection can be endlessly approximated as long as humans remain receptive to the enriching gifts of God.[77] In this context, it is important to note the high value Irenaeus places upon human becoming. Creatureliness is not understood as an unbridgeable gulf between being and becoming. On the contrary, it is understood in highly positive terms, as the means by which human beings in their state of becoming, both individually and throughout their history, may participate in ever greater degrees in the being of God. Indeed, an individual, though always characterised by the becoming of generate nature, in Irenaeus' words, 'gradually makes progress and comes to the Perfect, that is, comes to the ingenerate'.[78] Indeed, as has been observed, it is the distinction between creator and creature that forms the path to union.[79] In opposition to those who depreciate creation and seek to escape embodiment, Irenaeus understands creatureliness, defined by its becoming, as that which makes participatory progress possible. Furthermore, it is humanity itself that reveals God's glory in Adam and his descendants, and in the incarnation of God in Christ as we shall see. This positive valuation of physicality is summed up in one of the more frequently cited passages in Irenaeus' work: 'for living man is the glory of God, while the vision of God is the life of a man'.[80]

Divine Economy

A key notion in Irenaeus' understanding of the human–God participatory relationship is that of the divine economy, which is a means to conceptualise the being–becoming relationship in both a personal and world-historical

[75] *Adv. Haer.* IV.11.2. [76] *Adv. Haer.* IV.11.2. [77] *Adv. Haer.* IV.11.2.

[78] *Adv. Haer.* IV.38.3.

[79] Joseph Caillot, 'La grace de union selon saint Irénée', in *Penser la foi: recherches en théologie aujourd'hui: mélanges offert à Joseph Moingt*, ed. Joseph Doré and Christoph Theobald (Paris: Cerf, 1993), 395.

[80] *Adv. Haer.* IV.20.7.

framework.[81] In his own historical context, this was important in demonstrating that the God of the Old Testament and New Testament were indeed the same God, but at different stages of the management of the divine–human relationship. In the context of Irenaeus' thought, this notion of economy becomes a way to conceptualise the God–creation participatory relationship across the temporal history of creation, especially in relation to the story of human salvation. Irenaeus' employment of the term 'economy' is not limited in the way it is in its modern financial usage. Instead, reflecting its Greek etymology, it signified an intelligent and ordered plan for a household. For Irenaeus, working in the theological context of his times, it connotes a unified plan for the entirety of creation, with God as the master of the household that is creation. It is therefore also historical, accounting for the destiny of humankind taking in creation, fall, incarnation and salvation. It understands humans as moving gradually in stages towards ever greater participation in God, with God guiding this development in a way that continually offers ever greater participation in the image and likeness of God, despite the resistance humans often manifest towards it.

What necessitates the historical economy of participation is the created nature of humans themselves. Irenaeus likens the history of humankind to the history of a human life. Just as individuals must progress from infancy to maturity, so must humankind progress from spiritual infancy toward maturity. Humans cannot be equal to the being of God. Instead, they exist as part of a participatory history of becoming:

> created things, by the very fact that they had a beginning or origin, must by virtue of this be inferior as creatures to him who created them, for things recently made could not have been ingenerate. For this very reason that they are not ingenerate, they are inferior to the perfect being, because in as much as they are of more recent origin, they are infantile; and as such they are unaccustomed to, and unexercised in, perfected discipline. For just as a mother can give solid food to her infant, but the infant is not yet able to take the more substantial food, so also God could have given man perfection from the beginning, but man was incapable of receiving it, since he was still an infant.[82]

For Irenaeus, the participatory relationship between being and becoming, God and humankind, is characterised by progress or movement. This itself arises out of the asymmetry that exists between humans and God: 'because he is good, and has boundless riches, an everlasting kingdom, and an infinity of things to teach us', the human relationship to God will always be characterised by a dynamic

[81] Eric F. Osborn, *Irenaeus of Lyons* (Cambridge: Cambridge University Press), 58–61, 74–75.

[82] *Adv. Haer.* IV.38.1.

quality.[83] In relation to God, humans do not progress towards an end in the sense of completion, but towards the infinity of divine being itself. Human progress, therefore, is characterised by the infinite becoming of created humankind towards greater participation in the infinite being of God.[84]

The participatory relationship between divine being and human becoming in the divine economy leads Irenaeus to emphasise both the transcendence and immanence of God, and the importance of human materiality; both claims that aid in his opposition to the Gnostic and Marcionite positions. To articulate divine transcendence and immanence Irenaeus often employs the metaphor of God's hands.[85] Describing the immensity of divine reach, Irenaeus rhetorically asks 'who will understand his hand which measures the immense spaces, which by its own dimension stretches over the dimensions of the heavens, and which grasps in its palm the earth with the abysses, which contains within itself the breadth and length and depth below, and the height above, of the entire creation, whatever is seen, and heard and understood, and what is invisible?'[86] Here, the unfathomable immensity of God's hand transcends the breadth, length, and depth of human measure. However, in the same passage, Irenaeus goes on to articulate God's immanence in human life on the most intimate level: 'he is also with each one of us; for it says, I am a God at hand, and not a God far off.[87] Can a man hide himself in secret places so that I cannot see him? For his hand grasps all things. It is his hand that enlightens the heavens; it enlightens also the things under heaven; and it searches the minds and hearts[88] and is present in hidden and secret parts of ourselves, yet it nourishes and conserves us visibly'.[89] For Irenaeus, there is nowhere that God's hands do not reach. In their activity of enlightening all things, they are active in parts of humans unknown even to themselves, and known only to God, as well as those which are visible to us according to Irenaeus. It is on both the scale of cosmic transcendence and personal immanence that the participatory history of salvation unfolds.

The transcendence of God is something Irenaeus elaborates in terms of his epistemological claims, wherein truth must be understood as something that is received as opposed to something which is created by human beings. Critiquing the reasoning (here numerology) that was favoured by his adversaries, Irenaeus writes that 'all created things must be harmonized with the existing system of truth. For a rule does not come from numbers, but numbers from a rule; neither does God [come] from created things, but created things from God'.[90] Here

[83] *Adv. Haer.* II.28.3. [84] Osborn, *Irenaeus*, 82–85.
[85] *Adv. Haer.* III.21.10. See also 22.1; IV.praef.4; 20.1; 22.1; 39.2; V.1.3; 5.1–2; 6.1; 15.2–3; 28.4.
[86] *Adv. Haer.* IV.19.2. [87] Jeremiah 23:23. [88] Revelation 2:23. [89] *Adv. Haer.* IV.19.2.
[90] *Adv. Haer.* II.25.1.

Irenaeus is not taking up a fideist position, nor does he reject human learning or relativise it. Instead, he contextualises the pursuit of knowledge within a participatory framework which makes human understanding contingent upon its awareness of participation in the divine economy. The knowledge that is situated within a participatory frame recognises that it is part of a process of infinite unfolding, and that consequently it always remains approximate of the knowledge that it seeks. Articulated in the language already considered, knowing remains in a state of becoming relative to the knowledge of being that it desires.

Humans in the Participatory Economy: Image and Likeness

In his consideration of divine imminence, Irenaeus sets out the God–human relationship through the story of the creation of Adam, the fall, and the incarnation and salvific role of Christ, all within the context of the divine economy. As already elaborated, in opposition to his opponents, Irenaeus stresses the physicality of creation and the goodness of that creation. Rather than stressing any gulf between God and humans, even in the post-lapsarian context, Irenaeus emphasises God's immanent involvement in creation, and the necessity of creaturely existence for human participation in God, as opposed to considering it to be a barrier. To stress this physicality, Irenaeus emphasises the mud out of which Adam was made along with the previously described divine hands that moulded it into human form. He explains how 'the first-fashioned Adam got his substance from untilled and as yet a virgin soil . . . formed by God's hand'.[91] All humans share this physical, earthly origin, which establishes a relationship of receptivity between the divine and the human.[92] This participatory relationship is, as elsewhere, entirely asymmetrical: 'To follow the light', writes Irenaeus, 'means to receive light; those however, who are in the light do not themselves enlighten the light, but are enlightened and made resplendent by it'.[93] For Irenaeus, the glory of human beings is to remain in and preserve this participatory relationship, which allows humans to ever-approximate the divine likeness.

The notion of humans made in the image and likeness of God as described in Genesis is key for Irenaeus' conceptualisation of the divine economy and the process of approximation.[94] He returns again and again to the passage, 'Let us make humankind in our image, according to our likeness', indicating its importance to his theology.[95] Though his interpretation of the passage is not consistent across *Adversus Haerses*, in one important consideration of it, Irenaeus lays out

[91] *Adv. Haer.* III.21.10. [92] *Adv. Haer.* V.14.2. [93] *Adv. Haer.* IV.14.1.
[94] Osborn, *Irenaeus*, 196–99. [95] Genesis 1:26.

the relationship between image, likeness, and the role of the body and spirit, in making up the full human:

> It is he [man] who was made after God's image and likeness. But if the spirit is lacking to the soul, such a one is truly installed and, having been left carnal, he will be imperfect. He has the image of the handiwork but has not assumed the likeness through the spirit. Just as such a one is imperfect, so, if anyone takes away the image and spurns the handiwork, this can no longer be considered man, but either a part of man, as we have said, or something other than men. For the handiwork of the flesh by itself is not the perfect man but the body of man and a part of man. Neither is even the soul itself a man, but the soul of man and a part of man; Nor is the spirit man, for it is called spirit and not man. But the mingling and the union of all these makes the perfect man.[96]

Irenaeus goes on to provide examples of this perfect individual, describing those 'who speak with tongues through the spirit', and those who possess 'prophetic charism', as manifesting likeness along with image.[97]

In the case of Adam, 'God was able in the beginning to grant perfection to man; but man, having been recently made, could not receive it; nor, having received it, could he have comprehended it'.[98] That perfection is granted but not retained implicitly reflects the distinction between that of being and becoming considered earlier. On one hand, image is the entirely asymmetrical element of the participatory relationship over which humans lack any authority. It is the very idea of human in which individuals must participate to have their very existence (see Section 4). On the other hand, likeness is that part of the participatory relationship towards which human beings become, and in which humans choose to take part by divine grace. Following from the loss of Adamic perfection, incarnation made the perfection of divine likeness something that human beings could comprehend: 'And for this reason the Word of God, though he was perfect, became an infant together with and for man. Not for his own sake but because of humanity's infancy, thus he made himself contained so that humanity could grasp him'.[99] Here we see the full range of Irenaeus' understanding of the participatory economy as the means through which salvation occurs across creation.[100] Irenaeus' perspective on history ultimately takes a long view: 'All things were foreknown by the Father and will be effected by the Son, in the proper order and at the appropriate time'.[101] This slow process is for the benefit of human beings. 'Humankind', Irenaeus explains, 'needed to grow accustomed to bearing divinity, and God had to grow accustomed to dwelling in humankind'.[102] Elsewhere he

[96] *Adv. Haer.* V.6.1. [97] *Adv. Haer.* V.6.1. [98] *Adv. Haer.* IV.38.2.
[99] *Adv. Haer.* IV.38.2, see also V.16.2. [100] *Adv. Haer.* V.16.2, see also 36.1–3.
[101] *Adv. Haer.* III.16.7. [102] *Adv. Haer.* III.20.2.

states that this process of becoming accustomed to God is something that is required on the part of creation because it 'was necessary that humankind should first be fashioned, and that what was fashioned should be ensouled and thence receive the communion of the Spirit'.[103]

The fall was a turn away from the likeness component of the participatory relationship. What was to be achieved in the fullness of time in Irenaeus is reasoning, the likeness of God, was abandoned when it was seemingly offered immediately by the serpent in the Garden of Eden. It was through a kind of spiritual impatience, a desire to be fully like God, that the first humans fell away from participating in the divine likeness and were given over to death.[104] Irenaeus places the fall into the broad context of his participatory economy when he rhetorically asks:

> How, then, can he be a God who has not yet been made a man? How can he be perfect who has but recently being created, how can he be a mortal who in his mortal nature did not obey this maker? It is a fact that you must preserve the order of man and afterward partake of the glory of God. For you do not make God, but God makes you. So if you are the work of God, wait for the hand of your artificer, which will make all things in due time, as far as you are concerned who are created. Offer to him your heart pliable and docile, and guard the image according to which the artificer patterned you.[105]

This disposition of remaining pliable to the hands of God is one of remaining open to a participatory relationship with God. For Irenaeus, pliability is determinate of and necessary for salvation.[106] As the obedience of created reality to the hand of God that created it, pliability maintains the dynamism of the participatory relationship whose end is the justification and glorification of human beings made in the image and likeness of God. Irenaeus writes that 'God is the glory of humanity, but humanity is the vessel of God's working, of all his wisdom and power. Just as a physician proves himself among the sick, so God is manifested among human persons'.[107] To turn away from this relationship is to render oneself 'hardened' in Irenaeus' language, and thereby cutting off the voluntary part of the participatory relationship.[108] Articulating the contrasting roles of divine being and human becoming in the economy, Irenaeus explains that 'it is proper to God's likeness to make; but it is proper to man's nature to be made'.[109]

Incarnation and Recapitulation

The restoration of the possibility of humans to the state of becoming in relation to the divine likeness occurs through the incarnation, whose salvific

[103] *Adv. Haer.* V.12.2. [104] *Adv. Haer.* V.8.2. [105] *Adv. Haer.* IV.39.2.
[106] *Adv. Haer.* IV.39.2. [107] *Adv. Haer.* III.20.2. [108] *Adv. Haer.* IV.39.2.
[109] *Adv. Haer.* IV.39.2.

efficacy Irenaeus understands through the concept of recapitulation.[110] As *Adversus Haereses* explains, Christ, 'when he became incarnate and was made man, he recapitulated [recepitulavit] in himself the long unfolding of humankind, granting salvation by way of compendium [conpendio], that in Christ Jesus we may receive what we had lost in Adam, namely, to be according to the image and likeness of God'.[111] For Irenaeus, Christ's ability to gather together all things comes from both his eternality, shared with the Father, and from his temporality, through the incarnation. The notion of recapitulation is taken from Ephesians, which articulates how God through Christ has 'a plan for the fullness of time, to gather up all things in him, things in heaven and things on earth'.[112] The term itself is borrowed from rhetoric, having the meaning of summing up or gathering the main points of an argument into a summation. This rhetorical source comes through in Irenaeus' use of the word 'compendium'.[113]

In his treatment of salvation, Irenaeus does not emphasise the loss of a prelapsarian perfection, which he believes that humans in their infancy were unable to appreciate or understand. Instead, his emphasis is upon the restoration of humanity's participation in God particularly in terms of likeness. For Irenaeus, recapitulation accomplishes this by Christ's participation in every element of human life, both in general humanity, and particularly by retracing Adam's life. Christ passes through every age that humans do according to Irenaeus – from infancy to youth to adulthood – and in all of these he exemplifies the obedience of faith.[114] Irenaeus bases this in part upon the genealogy of Jesus found in Luke, which begins with Joseph and traces itself backwards to Adam.[115] Consequently, in Irenaeus' logic Christ recapitulates not just Adam but all of Adam's progeny.[116] To emphasise the recapitulatory relationship between the first and second Adam Irenaeus offers a set of parallels. For example, whereas the first human is made from untilled ground, Christ is born from a virgin's womb.[117] Furthermore, where Adam and Eve are disobedient, Mary, in the context of the Annunciation, and Christ, in the context of the temptation in the wilderness, are obedient.[118] Christ's obedience reaches its climax in the crucifixion where 'the Word of God himself, having become incarnate, was suspended on a tree'.[119] Irenaeus stresses the physical nature of the incarnation as a form of divine participation in human being. Irenaeus writes that 'the entire economy of our Lord's coming is for the sake of man. He

[110] Minns, *Irenaeus*, 108–12. [111] *Adv. Haer.* III.18.1. [112] Ephesians 1.8–10.
[113] Minns, *Irenaeus*, 108. [114] *Adv. Haer.* II.22.4–6; see also III.18.7; III.22.4.
[115] Luke. 3.23–38. [116] *Adv. Haer.* III.18.1; see also III.22.3.
[117] *Adv. Haer.* III.18.7; see also III.21.9. [118] *Adv. Haer.* III.18.7.
[119] *Adv. Haer.* V.18.1, see also V.16.3.

himself, therefore, had flesh and blood, and he recapitulated in himself not some other kind, but the father's original handiwork'.[120] Christ, like all human beings, is subject to mortality and all of the weaknesses that inhere in it. As a human being, he suffers the way other human beings suffer, and this, for Irenaeus, is the ultimate evidence of divine participation in human being. In defending the reality of God's incarnation against those who argue that God was not fully incarnate, he writes that 'if God did not suffer, we would owe him nothing', since the suffering of humans as created beings would be real, whilst the suffering of Jesus would only be an appearance.[121] However, the suffering of Christ is as real for Irenaeus as the suffering of any other human being; 'the Lord redeemed us by his own blood, gave his soul for our soul, his flesh for our flesh'.[122] It is by this suffering, writes Irenaeus, that the 'Son of God' becomes the 'Son of Man'.[123]

In Irenaeus' account of the incarnation, there is a double movement of descent and ascent. According to Irenaeus, God descends to humans, and humans are restored to God. 'He [Christ] brought God down to human beings through the spirit', Irenaeus writes, 'and lifted humankind up to God by his incarnation. In his coming to us he gives us incorruption, truly and firmly, through our communion with him'.[124] Throughout the *Adversus Haereses*, Irenaeus stresses how Christ's divinity is not something that is obscured by his humanity. Rather, it is through his humanity itself that divinity is revealed and revealed in a context which is passable and understandable to the limitations of human beings.[125] God's participation in the particularity of human beings through the recapitulation of incarnation moves away from more abstract considerations of the relation between God and creatures in general. With the incarnation, there is no great ontological gulf between divine being and the becoming of creation. Deeply influenced by the Gospel of John, Irenaeus stresses that Jesus as the Word is the creator, and as the incarnate Word, Christ, is the redeemer. This draws creation and salvation together in one complete reality:

> for it was necessary for him, becoming visible, to make manifest his form of the cross in everything, that he might demonstrate, by his visible form on the cross, his activity which is on the invisible level, for it is he who illumines the 'heights', that is, the things in heaven, and holds the 'deeps', which is beneath the earth, and stretches the 'length' from the east to the west, and who navigates the 'breadth' of the northern and southern regions, inviting the dispersed from all sides to the knowledge of the father.[126]

[120] *Adv. Haer.* V.14.2. [121] *Adv. Haer.* III.18.6. [122] *Adv. Haer.* V.1.1.
[123] *Adv. Haer.* III.18.6. [124] *Adv. Haer.* V.1.1. [125] *Adv. Haer.* IV.16.2; see also 6.3; 38.1.
[126] St. Irenaeus, *On the Apostolic Preaching: St Irenaeus of Lyons*, trans. John Behr, Popular Patristics Series 17 (Crestwood: St Vladimir's Seminary Press, 1997), 34.

Here, for Irenaeus, Christ is not to be understood as something apart from creation. Instead, the incarnation and the recapitulation it accomplishes change the nature of creation itself, marking it with the shape of the cross, and revolutionising the possibilities of becoming. Fundamentally, for Irenaeus, human participation in Christ is not something achieved forensically, in the sense that humans are attributed something which is not of themselves. 'Really', Irenaeus rhetorically asks, 'in what way could we be partakers of filial adoption, unless we had received through the Son participation in himself; unless his Word, having become flesh, had granted us communion in God?'[127] For Irenaeus, creation in general and human beings in particular are sanctified, or in Irenaeus's terminology brought into filial relation with God, with all the physical closeness that relational word entails, first by their very created nature, and second by the recapitulation of that nature in Christ.

Balthasar and Participatory Drama

There is a dramatic quality to Irenaeus' conceptualisation of the participatory relationship between God and creation in the history and life of humanity which can further elucidate the participatory dimension of incarnation and salvation. This drama of participation is not theatrical in the manner of entertainment, but in the sense that it is capable of presenting the human condition back to us in a form that invites its own insight into the nature of creaturely existence. The 20th-century Swiss theologian Hans Urs von Balthasar, among whose influences was Irenaeus, advocated such a dramatic view of the incarnation and salvation and as such his work offers a constructive compliment to Irenaeus' early Christian thought.[128] Balthasar is known for his sixteen-volume theological trilogy. The first part, *The Glory of the Lord* (*Herrlichkeit*, 7 vols., 1961–1967) considers God's self-disclosure in the form of a theological aesthetics. The second part, the *Theo-Drama* (*Theodramatik*, 5 vols., 1973–1983), attends to the dramatic encounter between God and humanity. The third part, the *Theo-Logic* (*Theologik*, 3 vols., 1985–1987), considers how the preceding observations can be conceptually transposed to the end of comprehension, proclamation, and contemplation.[129] In the *Theo-Drama*, Balthasar makes the claim that the categories of drama offer theology the capacity to convey the participatory

[127] *Adv. Haer.* III.18.7.

[128] Hans Urs von Balthasar, *Glory of the Lord: A Theological Aesthetics*, trans. Andrew Louth, et al. (San Francisco: Ignatius Press, 2006), II, 32–95.

[129] Hans Urs von Balthasar, 'Another Ten Years: 1975', trans. John Saward, in *The Analogy of Beauty: The Theology of Hans Urs von Balthasar*, ed. John Riches (Edinburgh: T. & T. Clark, 1986), 226.

nature of human being, characterised as it is by a continuing state of becoming, as unfolding upon the stage of creation:[130]

> For in the theatre man attempts a kind of transcendence, endeavoring both to observe and to judge his own truth, in virtue of a transformation – through the dialectic of the concealing-revealing mask – by which he tries to gain clarity about himself. Man himself beckons, invites the approach of a revelation about himself. Thus, parabolically, a door can open to the truth of the real revelation.[131]

Balthasar makes the case that the 'theo-praxy' of drama can best represent the divine–human encounter, capturing the spiritual experience of individuals.[132] Drama can 'express this in a form in which all the dimensions and tensions of life remain present instead of being sublimated in the abstractions of a "systematic" theology'.[133] This is an important point for the consideration of divine participation, which is a living relationship before it ever becomes part of a philosophical system or theological doctrine.

In the *Theo-Drama* humans are not only audience members. Though on the one hand they are passive participants by virtue of their ontological relationship with God, they are also 'thrust onto the stage' as active participants in the drama of their own salvation.[134] This passive–active duality corresponds respectively to the image and likeness distinction Irenaeus introduces, and indeed the general and particular forms of participation set out in the first section. As Balthasar puts it, 'God's revelation is not an object to be looked at: it is his action in and upon the world, and the world can only respond, and hence "understand", through action on *its* part'.[135] To support this assertion Balthasar relies upon the same Pauline language that Irenaeus employed concerning the old and new Adam. In the incarnation, Balthasar writes that 'what is created is not a new human being; the same nature that belonged to the old Adam is now, through the drama of the life, death and resurrection of Jesus, carried over into the state of the new Adam'.[136]

Balthasar explains that the incarnation reaches its fullness beyond the particular life of the historical Jesus. The mission of Christ has a scope, he claims, that may take not just 'a whole lifetime or even the entire world time, to carry it out'.[137] As such Christ's mission unfolds in the tension that characterises human

130 Hans Urs von Balthasar, *Theo-Drama: Theological Dramatic Theory: Three Volumes*, trans. Graham Harrison (San Francisco: Ignatius Press, 1988–92), I, 268–305.

131 *TD*, I, 12.

132 Mark Allen McIntosh, *Christology from Within: Spirituality and the Incarnation in Hans Urs von Balthasar* (Notre Dame: University of Notre Dame Press, 1996), 42–44, 55–57.

133 Balthasar, 'Another Ten Years', 226. 134 *TD*, II, 17. 135 *TD*, I.15. 136 *TD*, III, 38.

137 *TD*, III, 230.

participation itself: 'Having given freedom to the creature', writes Balthasar, 'God, as Creator, is always "involved" in the world, and this means that there is always a divine-human dramatic tension'.[138] Creation is a stage of divine–human encounter, where human participation unfolds in the activity of self-definition in relation to the incarnate God. The role which individuals play in this cosmic drama is something that Balthasar defines as 'a borderline concept in the dialectic of immanence and transcendence, nature and supernature . . . And Christianity shows the direction in which the answer is to be sought'.[139] Under this dramatic logic, Christ is present in every moment, enacted in the lives of individuals who have been 'touched, transformed and resettled' in him, and who participate in what is called the community of believers, the body of Christ.[140]

4 Participatory Being in Existence, Multiplicity and Analogy

Thus far we have come to see participation as something that is fundamentally relational in nature. The challenge with the relationship between God and creation is how to conceptualise the unique nature of this participatory relationship, which is so categorically distinct from all other relationships that adhere between creatures themselves. One way to address this is to consider the nature of God, the unique party in this relationship. If one is able to articulate a sense of divine nature in relation to creatures, then the challenge of conceptualisation becomes clearer. Participation is central to the thought of Thomas Aquinas (c. 1225–74), the foremost figure of 13th-century philosophy and theology. Aquinas begins with the unique nature of divine being, and from this addresses the question of how it is that creatures come to participate in this nature. In doing so he elaborates important elements of the participatory God–creature relationship in relation to existence, continuous creation, multiplicity, and analogy. For the last of these, we will also briefly engage the thought of the 20th-century theologian Erich Przywara (1899–1972) to examine the ontological dimensions of analogy.

Aquinas on Participation

Early in his life Aquinas became a member of the newly founded Dominican order, which sent him to Paris and later Cologne to study. He was appointed a master of theology and spent many of his most important years teaching theology in Paris. Aquinas, one of the greatest of the scholastic thinkers, drew inspiration from a great diversity of sources, foremost among them the Bible,

138 *TD*, I, 129. 139 *TD*, I, 120. 140 *TD*, III, 230–3; *TD*, III, 259.

Aristotle, Augustine, Pseudo-Dionysius, John of Damascus, and Boethius, to synthesize a new Christian philosophy.

Scholarship has recognised the importance of participation in his work since the mid 20th century, and indeed much of the contemporary interest in it has grown from considerations of Thomas' thought.[141] As one scholar has noted, for Aquinas, participation 'provides the general metaphysical framework of most of his theological, anthropological and ethical inquiries'.[142] In part, this follows from the fact that Aquinas was influenced by important participatory thinkers in the Neoplatonic tradition such as Pseudo-Dionysius and Proclus. Yet it also follows from the fact that he sought to think about theological topics in the context of life and practice, even when considering issues like participation, which can tend more towards abstract forms of speculation. Participation, a concept that is fundamentally about the relationship between creatures and God naturally lent itself to this practical concern.[143]

The Elements of Participation

As his thought evolved Aquinas would develop a unique innovation in the understanding of participation based upon existence that would ground his entire metaphysics. At the centre of his metaphysics is the challenge of understanding the dependent relation that creatures have upon God. In an early attempt at defining participation, Aquinas develops an initial definition and taxonomy of the different ways in which it might be conceptualised as a relationship of dependence. He undertakes this definition in his *An Exposition of the On the Hebdomads of Boethius*. In this text, Aquinas considers Boethius' exploration of how it is that creatures can be considered to be good by existence if they are not themselves the source of their own goodness. This provides the occasion for Aquinas to puzzle out the precise meaning and function of participation in detail, and to do so in relation to the overall question of God's being:

141 See Rudi te Velde, *Aquinas on God: The 'Divine Science' of the Summa Theologiae* (Aldershot: Ashgate, 2006), 139–46; Jan Aertsen, *Nature and Creature: Thomas Aquinas's Way of Thought* (Leiden: Brill, 1988), 122–27; John F. Wippel, *The Metaphysical Thought of Thomas Aquinas: From Finite Being to Uncreated Being* (Washington, DC: Catholic University of America Press, 2000), 94–131; Cornelio Fabro, *La nozione metafisica di partecipazione: secondo S. Tommaso d'Aquino* (Torino: Societa editrice internazionale, 1950); Louis-Bertrand Geiger, *La participation dans la philosophie de St. Thomas d'Aquin* (Paris: J. Vrin, 1942); W. Norris Clarke, 'The Meaning of Participation in St. Thomas', *Proceedings of the American Catholic Philosophical Association*, 26 (1952): 147–57.

142 Velde, *Aquinas on God*, 123.

143 Andrew Davison, *Participation in God: A Study in Christian Doctrine and Metaphysics* (Cambridge: Cambridge University Press, 2019), 7.

> For 'to participate' is, as it were, 'to grasp a part' [Est autem participare quasi partem capere]. And, therefore, when something receives in a particular way that which belongs to another in a universal way, it is said 'to participate' in that, as human being is said to participate in animal because it does not possess the intelligible structure of animal according to its total commonality; and in the same way, Socrates participates in human. And similarly, too, a subject participates in accident, and matter in form, because a substantial form, or an accidental one, which is common by virtue of its own intelligible structure, is determined to this or that subject. And similarly, too, an effect is said 'to participate' in its own cause, and especially when it is not equal to the power of its cause, as for example, if we should say that 'air participates in the light of the sun' because it does not receive that light with the brilliance it has in the sun.[144]

Here Aquinas outlines differing manifestations of the participatory relationship, which can respectively be designated as the relationship between universal and particular, form and subject, and cause and effect. Aquinas has many discussions of participation in differing contexts throughout his work that further elucidate the contrasting relationship between God and creation.[145] In one instance he writes of participation in terms of a contrast between perfection and partial, where 'whatever is participated is determined to the mode of that which is participated and is thus possessed in a partial way and not according to every mode of perfection'.[146] Similarly, Aquinas writes of participation in terms of an infinite–finite relationship, where 'what is participated is not received in the one participating according to its entire infinity but in the manner of a particular'.[147] From these examples, though the elements vary, we can see that the participatory relationship as described has three common elements: (a) a source that possesses perfection completely and totally, (b) a participant that has the perfection partially and restrictedly, and (c) the relationship, characterised by reception and dependence of the participant upon the source for the participated perfection.[148] We can now consider the role of each of these elements in greater detail as they are examined in Aquinas' thought, first in an abstract source-participant context, and then in terms of the God–creation relationship.

---

[144] St. Thomas Aquinas, *An Exposition of the on the hebdomads of Boethius*, trans. Janice L. Schultz and Edward A. Synan (Washington, DC: Catholic University of America Press, 2001), 19.

[145] W. Norris Clarke, *Explorations in Metaphysics: Being-God-Person* (Notre Dame: University of Notre Dame Press, 1994); Clarke, *Meaning of Participation*, 93.

[146] *SCG* I.32.7. All quotations from *Summa contra Gentiles* are from the edition translated by Anton C. Pegis, et al. (Notre Dame: University of Notre Dame Press, 1975).

[147] St. Thomas Aquinas, *Commentary on the Book of Causes*, prop. 2, n. 30, trans. Charles R. Hess, Richard C. Taylor, and Vincent A. Guagliardo (Washington, DC: Catholic University of America Press, 1996), 33.

[148] Clarke, *Meaning of Participation*, 93.

In the context of the perfect source–participant relationship, the source (a), which possesses perfection completely and totally, cannot receive its perfection from another source. As the ultimate source in this relationship, it must possess perfection by necessity. The perfection is therefore its essence. Aquinas elaborates this by examining predication, of which he writes there are two forms: 'There are two ways to attribute something to a thing: *essentially*, and by *participation*. Light, for instance, is attributed to an illuminated body by participation, but if there were a separate light, then it would be attributed to that light essentially'.[149] Here we can see two forms of predication: that which is predicated of the source is by its essence, and that which is predicated of the participant is by its participation. The essential form of predication reveals further facets when we examine the source in comparison to the participant. First, it tells us that the source is simple in nature, as Aquinas writes, 'For that which is something in its entirety does not participate in it but is essentially identical with it, whereas that which is not something in its entirety but has this other thing joined to it, is said properly to participate in that thing'.[150] Simplicity also yields the necessary unique nature of this source, since 'a common nature, if considered in separation from things, can be only one, although there can be a plurality of things possessing that nature'.[151] Following from this, it is the case that if there appeared to be two sources with the same perfection, they would in fact not be distinguishable, and hence would be one unique unity. A further consequence of this is that the source has the quality of the infinite, since 'absolutely infinite being cannot be twofold'.[152] Consequently, according to Aquinas' reasoning, the basic metaphysical structure of the source must be that its predicate is its essence, and that it is simple, unique and infinite in nature.

The nature of the second component, the participant (b) who has perfection partially and restrictedly, is broadly the opposite of the perfect source (a), being composite and multiple. As we can see from the above distinction concerning predication, it cannot possess a perfection by essence. Instead, it must participate in the source in a limited or contracted way. In a passage that describes this with some economic clarity, Aquinas writes that 'whenever something is attributed to a thing by participation, there must be something else there besides what is participated. Hence, in the case of every creature, the creature that has existence is other than the existence it has'.[153] Here, the composite nature of the participation comes from its being composed of, at minimum, the perfection

149 II, q. 2, a1 *Thomas Aquinas's Quodlibetal Questions*, trans. Brian Davies and Turner Nevitt (Oxford: Oxford University Press, 2020), italics added; also *ST* 1a.3.4.rep.

150 St. Thomas Aquinas, *Commentary on the Metaphysics of Aristotle*, trans. John Patrick Rowan (Chicago: H. Regnery, 1961), I Met. Lect. 10, 154.

151 *SCG* II.52.3. 152 *SCG* II.52.3. 153 *Quodlibetal Questions*, II.q.2.a.1.

received, and the subject that receives and limits it. Consequently, we can see that the basic metaphysical nature of the (b) participant is distinct in nature from the (a) source.

The relationship (c) between the (a) source and (b) participant is characterised by reception and dependence. In the case of the first of these, Aquinas makes use of a modified version of Aristotle's distinction between act and potency.[154] The source is understood as the act, which by its simple and unique nature cannot limit itself. The participant is the potency, which naturally imposes limitations on the act received because of its composite and limited nature. In characterising this receptive relationship, Aquinas writes that 'whatever participates in a thing is compared to the thing participated in as act is related to potentiality, since by that which is participated the participator is actualised in such a way'.[155] Together, act and potency allow Aquinas to account for the unity of the composite nature of the participant. Furthermore, it reveals the asymmetrical dependence of the recipient upon the source. The default state of participants in their relationship with the source is one of non-being: 'Non being is prior to being in the thing which is said to be created . . . [I]f the created thing is left to itself, it would not exist, because it only has its being from the causality of the higher cause. What a thing has in itself and not from something else is naturally prior in it to that which it has from something else'.[156] The question as to what things have in themselves can only be answered by moving this consideration of the participatory relationship out of this abstract context, and into the concrete participatory relationship of God and creatures.

Existence and Participation

Having treated participation in abstract terms, we now explore how, in the metaphysics of divine participation, (a) the source is God, (b) the participant is creation (or the individual creatures that make up creation), and (c) the relation between both is asymmetrical.

In terms of God having the character of the source, Aquinas writes that 'God exists by nature, and all other beings participate'.[157] Essence therefore is essentially predicated of God, as opposed to being predicated of God by

154 Aristotle, *Metaphysics,* 1017a 35–b 9; 1045b 28–2052a 12; *Physics*, 184a9-192b5.

155 *SCG* II.53.4; see also *SCG* I.18.2.

156 St. Thomas Aquinas, *Aquinas on Creation: Writings on the 'Sentences' of Peter Lombard, Book 2, Distinction 1, Question 1*, trans. Steven E. Baldner and William E. Carroll (Toronto: Pontifical Institute of Mediaeval Studies, 1997), 74–75.

157 *ST* 1a.4.3.ad3. (modified) – All *Summa Theologiae* quotes from the edition edited by David Bourke, 60 vols. (Cambridge: Cambridge University Press, 2006).

participation. Following from God's essence being that of existence, divine being must be understood as supremely existent and supremely undivided: 'Both characteristics belong to God. He exists supremely, because he has not acquired an existence which his nature has then determined, but is subsistent existence itself, which is in no way determined. He is also supremely undivided, because as we have seen, he is altogether simple, not divided in any way, and this neither actually nor potentially'.[158] Further, in terms of the act-potency structure, God is the supreme act: 'the most perfect thing of all is to exist, for everything else is potential compared to existence. Nothing achieves actuality except it exists, and the act of existing is therefore the ultimate actuality of everything, and even of every form'.[159] Elsewhere, stressing God's simplicity, Aquinas writes that 'In God there is no potency. Therefore, there is no composition in him'.[160] Finally, the asymmetrical creator–creature relationship is vividly expressed by Aquinas through the image of undiminishing sunlight illuminating the air: 'Now every creature may be compared to God, as the air is to the sun which enlightens it. For as the sun possesses light by its nature, and as the air is enlightened by sharing the sun's nature, so God alone is being in virtue of his own essence, since his essence is his existence, whereas every creature has being by participation, so that its essence is not its existence'.[161]

Since God is the ultimate actuality of everything, all creatures that have existence have it from God through participation. Aquinas sums up this relationship as follows:

> everything that is at all real is from God. For when we encounter a subject which participates in a reality then this reality must needs be caused there by a thing which possesses it of its nature . . . Now we have already shown when treating of the divine simplicity, that God is sheer existence subsisting of his very nature [ipsum esse per se subsistens]. And such being, as we have also noted, cannot but be unique . . . for its repetition depends on there being many receiving subjects. We are left with the conclusion that all things other than God are not their own existence but participate in existence.[162]

Through participation creatures have both their being and essence. Being is that by which the creature fundamentally exists and continues to exist, and essence is that which determines the particularity of an individual creature. Creatures receive both of these from God simultaneously. Aquinas writes that 'God at the same time gives being and produces that which receives being, so that it does not follow that his action requires something already in

[158] *ST* 1.11.3. [159] *ST* 1a.4.2.ad.3. [160] *SCG* I.18.2. [161] *ST* 1.104.1.
[162] *ST* 1.44.1.resp.

existence'.[163] Here we see that in the creation of an individual creature we have at the same time the creation of its existence in general, and the particular nature of that existence, with both essentially related in the individual creature. A creature's existence is defined by the limitations placed upon it by essence, and creaturely being achieves its actuality through the particular essence that it receives. Any knowledge that humans have of these particular essences arises out of participation in divine perfection itself. According to Aquinas:

> God can know all things in himself with a knowledge of what is proper to each. For the nature proper to each thing consists in its participation in the divine perfection in some degree. But God would not know himself perfectly if he did not know all the ways in which his perfection can be participated by other things; nor would he know perfectly the nature of existence if he did not know all the degrees of existence. Hence it is clear that God knows all things in what is proper to each and makes them different from one another.[164]

Creatures always exist in their own particular way by participating in divine perfection in varying degrees that are appropriate to them. The function of essence is to contain and contract being into its creaturely particularity. Aquinas writes that, 'it follows strictly that all things which are diversified by their diverse participation in existence, so that some are fuller beings than others, are caused by one first being which simply is in the fullest sense of the word'.[165] This activity of participating in varying degrees and containing and contracting being are the source of the multiplicity that characterises creation in general, and simultaneously the unity that draws that multiplicity back together in the perfection of God.

Continuous Creation

With this account of participatory existence now set out, we can now look at how the multiplicity of creation and the language used to describe it are also participatory. However, foremost we should examine what we might call the fundamental consequence of participation in being. In the participatory relationship, as Aquinas puts it: 'God exists in everything; not indeed as a part of their substance or as an accident, but as an agent is present to that in which its action is taking place'.[166] Creation derives from and continues to depend upon God in a 'profoundly interior' way. However, at the same time, creatures are in no way continuous with God or made of God. This intimate presence is often

---

[163] St. Thomas Aquinas, *On the Power of God: Quaestiones Disputatae de Potentia Dei*, trans. Fr. Lawrence Shapcote (Westminster: Newman Press, 1952), I, rep. 17.

[164] *ST* 1.14.6; cf. *Quodlibetal Questiones*, 1 54. [165] *ST* 1.44.1.resp. [166] *ST* 1a.8.1.resp.

referred to as continuous creation (creatio continua), which can be contrasted both with pantheism, where creatures are part of God, and deism, where creatures are self-sustaining once created by God. Aquinas' formulation makes it clear that God is present to all creatures both as their cause and as their continuation:

> God is causing this effect [i.e. existence] in things not just when they begin to exist, but all the time they are maintained in existence . . . During the whole period of a thing's existence, therefore, God must be present to it, and present in a way in keeping with the way in which the thing possesses its existence. Now existence is more intimately and profoundly interior to things than anything else, for everything as we said is potential when compared to existence. So God must exist and exist intimately in everything.[167]

Here, Aquinas essentially offers a metaphysical account that is entirely in keeping with creatio ex nihilo, which we can now see as fundamental to the God–creature participatory relationship. Creation is unlike change. It is the action of making something from nothing, giving the creature foremost participation in being, and second, participation in essence. However, another dimension of the participatory relationship now comes into relief through this understanding of creation. Since all creatures have their initial and continuing existence through God, we come to see that creation is not a singular act, but a sustaining activity.

Multiplicity

The continued participatory relationship between creatures and God also shapes Aquinas' understanding of creaturely multiplicity. Rather than seeing the profound diversity of nature as a fall away from the unity of the divine One, Aquinas understands it as fundamentally a result of divine intention. The singular nature of divine goodness requires multiplicity to be communicated and represented in a form which human beings can cognize. Therefore, multiplicity represents the endless dimensionality of infinite divine goodness participated in finite form. Aquinas writes that:

> [The] distinctiveness and plurality of things is because the first agent, who is God, intended them. For he brought things into existence so that his goodness might be communicated to creatures and re-enacted through them. And because one single creature was not enough, he produced many and diverse, so that what was wanting in one expression of divine goodness might be supplied by another, for goodness, which in God is single and altogether, in

[167] *ST* 1a.8.1,resp.

> creatures is multiple and scattered. Hence the whole universe less incompletely than one alone shares and represents his goodness.[168]

Since multiplicity is the means to communicate divine goodness, the greater the multiplicity of creaturely reality, the greater the communication of divine goodness.

Since God is continuously and intimately present in all creation, coming to know creation is a way for humans to come to know God. The study of nature, whether through the arts or sciences, is not a secular or profane activity, but one which is sacred in itself. Creation makes divine wisdom intelligible to human beings: 'God brought things into being by his wisdom; wherefore the Psalm declares: "thou hast made all things in wisdom." Hence, from reflection upon God's works we are able to infer his wisdom, since, by a certain communication of his likeness, it is spread abroad in the things he has made. For it is written: "he poured her out," namely, wisdom, "upon all his works"'.[169] The proper object of human intellect is continuous creation since, as Aquinas explains, 'the intellect . . . rises to the limited knowledge it has of invisible things by way of the nature of visible things'.[170] Only through knowledge of the many in all of their various forms of limited being can humans come to greater knowledge of God, the source of all being.

Analogy

Since God is encountered through participation in creation, this naturally generates the question of how human words and concepts, which are fundamentally orientated towards the creaturely world, can have the capacity to disclose a divine subject.

Aquinas' answer is found in the capacity of analogy to steer a middle course between the extremes of univocity, which entails the pure identity of meaning between the words used of objects, and an equivocity, which entails an opposing ambiguity of meaning in words. Aquinas writes that: 'words are used neither univocally nor purely equivocally of God and creatures, but analogically, for we cannot speak of God at all except in the language we use of creatures, and so whatever is said both of God and creatures is said in virtue of the order that creatures have to God as their source and cause in which all the perfections of things pre-exist transcendentally'.[171]

This understanding of analogy is framed by Aquinas' participatory metaphysics. God's nature is radically other in the sense that it is not a thing among other things as we have seen. Instead, it is the very source and sustenance of all

168 *ST* 1.47.1.resp. 169 *SCG* 2.2.2; Psalm [103: 24] Ecclesiastes 1: 10.
170 *ST* 1a.84.7.resp. 171 *ST* 1a.15.5.resp.

extant things and their individual particularity. Nevertheless, because God is intimately present in all creation through this participatory relationship, creation by its very nature must express something of its divine source. Commenting upon this, Aquinas writes that:

> in this life we do not see the essence of God, we only know him from creatures; We think of him as their source, and then as surpassing them all and as lacking anything that is merely creaturely. It is the knowledge we have of creatures that enables us to use words to refer to God, so these words do not express the divine essence as it is in itself.[172]

According to Aquinas, the creaturely reality that words name has its source and maintenance in God. Nevertheless, God's surpassing nature, whose perfection does not have the limitations that characterise participating creatures, also restricts the capacities of these words to express the divine essence.[173] This restricted use forms the basis for the analogical use of language, which constitutes a middle path between equivocal and univocal predication. According to Aquinas, when we use a word to describe both God and creatures it is neither univocal nor equivocal. Instead, the relation is analogical, which signifies 'different relations to some one thing'.[174]

Language concerning God and creatures is analogous because the perfections of creatures exist in God perfectly. Consequently, to say that a person is good and God is good is to use the word good analogously because creatures have a likeness to God. The nature of this likeness is not that both God and creatures participate, in a concept called goodness. Rather, God is transcendently and perfectly good in God's self. Creatures therefore are like God when they participate in the certain likeness of God. There is no common abstract quality or form that enables both creatures and God to be good. God is the source of goodness that makes possible the analogical naming of diverse creatures that participate in divine goodness. It is in this way that we name God from creatures since creatures, having their source in God, share a likeness to God as effects of the divine creator.

When humans use the word good to describe God, the concept of good being used is the human understanding of a divine perfection, which by its nature is limited. Human beings do not have a full command of the perfection of good, however the way in which the word is used accords with how goodness is encountered in creation. To account for this, Aquinas makes a distinction

[172] *ST* 1a.13.1.resp.

[173] *ST* 1a.12.12; Fran O'Rourke, *Pseudo-Dionysius and the Metaphysics of Aquinas* (Leiden: Brill, 1992), 31–42; Velde, *Aquinas on God*, 76–107.

[174] *ST* 1a.13.6.resp.

between what a word signifies (res significata) and the way, or mode, by which a word is used to signify (modus significandi).[175] God is named from creatures, however the names themselves have their source in the creator. Put in terms of participation, all creatures participate in God, and the names derived from their participation relate back to God as the source that participates them. God is goodness as opposed to God having goodness. Creatures receive this goodness in multiple and particular ways by God's continuous creative action, and the multiplicity of goodness revealed in numerable creatures and ways deepens this knowledge of divine goodness.

Przywara and the Analogy of Being

The logic of analogy also extends beyond language, to being itself. Creation may be understood to exist as an ontological analogy through participation in divine being which exists in itself. There has been considerable scholarly debate as to whether Aquinas held this position himself, with some interpreters maintaining that analogy has a purely linguistic function in Aquinas' thought.[176] However, Aquinas' writing bears out an ontological version of analogy in addition to linguistic analogy. In considering the issue of whether creatures can be considered to be like God through participation, Aquinas argues that they indeed can, thereby extending his analogical considerations into an ontological context. At the same time, creation is an effect of God, and as such the likeness it bears to its divine source is a remote one. Aquinas writes that the likeness that is shared between God and creature 'will present the sort of analogy that holds between all things because they have existence in common. And this is how things receiving existence from God resemble him; for precisely as things possessing existence, they resemble the primary and universal source of all existence'.[177]

The 20th-century Jesuit theologian Erich Przywara built upon this position, using it to diagnose and avert the problems that characterise much of modern philosophy in his magnum opus *Analogia entis* (1932). For Przywara, in the same way that linguistic analogy provides a middle path between the extremes of equivocal and univocal linguistic meaning, ontological analogy does the

---

[175] *ST* 1a.13.3.resp.

[176] David Burrell, *Analogy and Philosophical Language* (New Haven: Yale University Press, 1973), 119ff.; David Burrell, *Aquinas: God and Action* (London: Routledge, 1979); Ralph McInerny, *The Logic of Analogy: An Interpretation of St. Thomas* (The Hague: Martinus Nijhoff, 1961); Ralph McInerny, *Studies in Analogy* (The Hague: Martinus Nijhoff, 1968); Ralph McInerny, *Aquinas and Analogy* (Washington, DC: Catholic University of America Press, 1996), 152ff.

[177] *ST* 1a.4.3.rep. See also *On the Principles of Nature*, IV.33.24; *Commentary on Aristotle's Metaphysics*, IV.535.

same by offering a metaphysical middle way. In the context of what has been termed his phenomenological approach, Przywara sets out to demonstrate how totalizing philosophical systems are inadequate to their task without their opposing counterpart system.[178] He makes this point by comparing what he understands to be the two broad approaches that characterise philosophy. On the one hand is a noetic approach that attempts to explicate reality from the standpoint of being, and on the other an ontic approach, that attempts to do so from consciousness. As it turns out, neither position is capable of offering a pure starting point. Instead, each ends up requiring the other, reflecting the analogical nature of created being itself.[179]

Przywara, building upon Aquinas' assertion that creaturely being and essence have their source in God and not in themselves, argues that any philosophical position must take account of this creaturely reality. The failure to do so results in the oscillation between either position that distinguishes much of modern philosophy, with its characteristic tension between an a priori and an a posteriori metaphysics, or transcendental metaphysics and metaphysical transcendentalism.[180] Analogical metaphysics is able to provide this by steering a middle way that accounts for human nature that is both in existence, yet has its essence beyond it. This is communicated in Przywara's important, yet somewhat gnomic, concept of 'essence *in*-and-*beyond*-existence'.[181] Building upon what is set out by Aquinas earlier in this section, namely that creaturely participation in essence makes a creature what it is, this relationship constitutes the essence '*in*' the creature. However, essence is present through participation, with its absolute reality remaining with God, and this is '*beyond*' the creature's individual existence. As such, Przywara argues that theology naturally arises from philosophical consideration.

Przywara goes on to articulate that the theological absolute is not the absolute of philosophy, which is posited and determined by creaturely concepts. Instead, God transcends philosophical conceptualisation yet reveals divinity in creation. As such Przywara describes God as 'God beyond-and-in the creature', in the same manner that characterizes creaturely being as essence-in-and-beyond existence. This affirms both philosophical approaches, and equally suspends them. As a consequence, participatory reality of creaturely existence is fundamentally dynamic. Creaturely being occupies a 'suspended middle', a unity of movement, that oscillates back and forth.[182] Equally, he describes creaturely being as 'a rhythmic middle', and as such inherently mysterious since it cannot be mastered by any philosophical concept.[183]

[178] Erich Przywara, *Analogia Entis: Metaphysics, Original Structure and Universal Rhythm*, trans. John R. Betz and David Bentley Hart (Grand Rapids: William B. Eerdmans, 2014), 62.

[179] Przywara, *Analogia Entis,* 119–24. [180] Przywara, *Analogia Entis*, 125–31; 132–53.

[181] Przywara, *Analogia Entis*, 158. [182] Przywara, *Analogia Entis*, 159.

[183] Przywara, *Analogia Entis*, 210.

Ontological analogy, therefore, is the being of the individual creature by its participatory nature which points beyond itself to what truly is. Przywara comments that 'analogy as a participatory being-related-above-and-beyond, has as its profounder premise and *analogy as the self-imparting-relation-from-above* of the divine identity of the Is [Analogie als teilgebendes Sich-von-oben-hinein-beziehen]'.[184] Theology is always present in philosophy, since its subject is always beyond itself to its reality in God. Analogy is fundamentally dynamic, a representation of the creature's condition back to itself. As such it echoes the conclusions of Irenaeus, and equally points us toward Cusa in the next section, who writes of the capacity of art to re-present this state of created reality back to us.

5 Participatory Knowing, Naming and Creating

In the previous sections of this text, we have examined the participatory relationship primarily in terms of God's activity of creation, salvation, and sustaining being. In this section, we will look at participation from a more actively human-sided perspective. For this we turn first to the 15th-century German bishop Nicholas of Cusa (Nicholas Cusanaus, 1401–1464), whose philosophical and theological speculation, based upon the absolute transcendence and immanence of God, demonstrates how deeply participatory human activity is on the most quotidian level. With Cusa we see that naming, knowing and making, all acts of human artifice, are participatory in their very nature. In terms of these activities, we will give special attention to art, which has the particular capacity of performatively demonstrating our own act of participation back to us in the activity of artistic creation itself. This is illustrated in Cusa, but also by later Romantic thought, for which the activity of aesthetic creation had particular importance as a grammar for the transcendent, and for this, we will turn specifically to the key Romantic thinkers of Friedrich Schlegel (1772–1829) and Samuel Taylor Coleridge (1772–1834).

Nicholas of Cusa

Nicholas of Cusa is sometimes referred to as a transitional figure between the medieval period and modernity. In part this is due to his bringing together of Italian humanist thought and the broader tradition of medieval Christian Platonism. He played an active role in the life of the church, taking a degree in Canon law, playing a role in debates concerning the extent of papal ecclesiastical authority, and becoming a bishop. What makes his thought stand out in

[184] Przywara, *Analogia Entis*, 214.

the context of this study is the important consideration of the human role in the participatory divine–human relationship.

In this section, we will focus on artifice, the creation of something by skill or craftsmanship. On the one hand, this term is useful because it differentiates the human activity of creation from the divine activity of creation set out in Section 2. Yet on the other hand, we must distinguish artifice from the modern use of the term, where to call the activity of making 'artifice' is to give it something of a negative connotation. This arises out of a context where human artifice is placed in opposition to something which is natural. Artifice therefore becomes a strategy or device that intends to present the human made as natural when in fact it is not. This in itself reveals an implicit assumption of an opposition between the human activity of making, whether by means of intellectual or physical constructs, and nature's making of itself. However, in the context of Cusa's philosophy, this nature/culture distinction is not present since all of nature and all of culture cannot help but participate in the oneness of God. In fact, in the context of Cusa's thought, one might call nature, or creation, God's artifice, and human cognitive constructions along with the physical activity of making artifacts, human forms of artifice. By considering the activities of naming, knowing and creating, we can come to see how 'all human arts are "images" of the infinite divine art'.[185] However, first we must foreground this consideration with the epistemological and metaphysical doctrine at the heart of Cusa's thought: the doctrine of ignorance.

De Docta Ignorantia is Cusa's most substantive philosophical work, based upon an understanding of the consequences of divine immanence and transcendence, laying the foundations for much of his later thought. Cusa terms the infinite nature of God the 'maximum', which is 'that than which there cannot be anything greater'.[186] Nothing exists outside of the maximum; its character is oneness. The oneness of the maximum entails that it is free from all relation, contraction, and imposition, as nothing may be relative to it, derived from it, or compounded with its all-encompassing nature. 'The infinite qua infinite, is unknown', writes Cusa, 'for it escapes all comparative relation'.[187] Cusa then proceeds to consider the coincidence of opposites between the maximum and minimum. The 'minimum' is defined as 'that than which there cannot be

[185] *DM* 2.59. All quotations from *Idiota de Mente* are from the translation by Jasper Hopkins, *Nicholas of Cusa on Wisdom and Knowledge* (Minneapolis: A. J. Banning Press, 1996); modified following the text: *Nicolai de Cusa Opera Omnia jussu et auctoritate Academicae Litterarum Heidelbergensis* (Leipzig-Hamburg: Meiner, 1932–2007).

[186] *DI* 1.2.5. All quotations from *De Docta Ignorantia* are from the translation by Jasper Hopkins, *Nicholas of Cusa on Learned Ignorance: A Translation and an Appraisal of de Docta Ignorantia* (Minneapolis: A. J. Banning Press, 1985).

[187] *DI* 1.1.3.

a lesser'.[188] Cusa articulates its coincidence with the maximum in relation to quantity: 'For maximum quantity is maximally large; and minimum quantity is maximally small. Therefore, if you free maximum and minimum from quantity – by mentally removing large and small – you will see clearly that maximum and minimum coincide'.[189] Both the maximum and the minimum are characterised by the indivisible oneness of divinity. It is in this manner that Cusa demonstrates the total transcendence of God through maximality and the total imminence of God through minimality. There is nothing between the maximum and minimum that does not participate in God.

Neither the maximum nor the minimum can be circumscribed by understanding in any conventional way. 'If we can fully attain unto this, writes Cusa, we can attain unto learned ignorance'.[190] The learned character of this kind of ignorance differentiates it from philosophical scepticism because it does not deny the possibility of knowledge. Indeed, inherent in the notions of maximum and minimum is the requirement to go beyond the negation of the possibility of the total knowledge of God and affirm knowledge of God through the participatory nature of the God–creation relationship. Here, the mystical component of Cusa emerges in the Neoplatonic dialectics at the heart of his thought. Metaphysically, divine presence saturates and encompasses all creatures without being limited to or circumscribed by them. Intellectually, as the undifferentiated and unlimited unity, God transcends all thought, yet simultaneously all thought is immanent to God, and therefore participates in the divine. As Cusa puts it, 'the unattainable oneness of truth is known by means of a conjecturing otherness; and the conjecturing otherness is known in and through a most simple oneness of truth'.[191] For humans, engaged in the world as we are, betwixt and between the maximum and the minimum, it is 'the case that our entire knowledge consists of participation in the divine actuality with a degree of potency'.[192] We experience these differing potencies, which we can also call degrees of approximation to the divine, in the day-to-day activities of naming, knowing and making.

Naming

The first activity of human artifice is naming, which Cusa describes as a 'power present in us which enfolds conceptually the exemplars of things'.[193] For Cusa, objects are only able to enter into our knowledge by means of the designations we provide for them, and naming is the 'medium through which the object can

[188] *DI* 1.4.11. [189] *DI* 1.4.11. [190] *DI* 1.1.4.

[191] *DC* 1.*Prol*. 2. All quotations from *De Coniecturis* are from the translations by Jasper Hopkins, *Nicholas of Cusa: Metaphysical Speculations: Volume Two* (Minneapolis: A. J. Banning Press, 2000).

[192] *DI* 1.2.56. [193] *DM* 2.58.

replicate a form of itself, or a sign of itself'.[194] For Cusa, 'the imposition of a name occurs by the operation of reason'.[195] It is the function of reason to take the information offered by the senses and distinguish, harmonise, and differentiate it. Through the activity of naming, the external world comes to furnish the mind. Aligning himself towards the Aristotelian-Thomistic position (see Section 4), and thereby differentiating himself from a more traditionally Platonic one (see Section 2), Cusa writes that 'in our reason there is nothing that was not previously in our senses'.[196]

Consequently, the names with which reason is concerned, both generic and specific, are entities of reason which follow from perception, and are made for the purpose of harmonising and differentiating perceptible objects. Initially, this might seem to threaten equivocal subjectivity. Cusa comments that 'we name one thing by one name, for a certain reason; and the very same thing by another, for another reason. Moreover, one language has names that are more suitable, whereas another language has names that are cruder and less suitable. In this way, I see that since the suitability of names admits of more or less, the precise name is not known'.[197] Yet, this is not an anti-realist position. Instead, based upon the concept of the maximum in the doctrine of learned ignorance, and in correlation with the notion of naming, Cusa maintains that 'there is only one, most simple infinite form, which in all things *shines forth* as the most adequate exemplar of each in every formable thing'.[198] There is not, for example, as was the case with Augustine, a heaven of heavens where the divine ideas or forms created by God reside (see Section 2). Rather, all particulars participate in one, simple, infinite form. The same is true of language: 'there is one ineffable word, which is the precise name of all things insofar as these things are captured by a name through the operation of reason. In its own manner this ineffable name shines forth in all names'.[199] Consequently, whilst our own internal artifice may be the originator of the names we apply to things, all these names participate in the one ineffable word, and consequently the one most simple form.

Relating naming back to the maximum, Cusa quotes Hermes Trismegistus who, he writes, 'rightly says: "Since God is the totality of things, no name is proper to him; for either he would have to be called by every name or else all things would have to be called by His name"; for in his simplicity, he enfolds the totality of things'.[200] Human language, which may seem arbitrary, and in fact, as Cusa articulates, in some ways is in its various application by us, cannot help but participate in the truth since its artifice is by necessity enfolded into divine oneness, and human made language 'shines forth' that oneness. This also gives

[194] *Comp.* 4.8. Translation from Jasper Hopkins, *On Wisdom and Knowledge* (see above note 1).
[195] *DM* 2.64. [196] *DM* 2.64. [197] *DM* 2.58. [198] *DM* 2.67. Emphasis added.
[199] *DM* 2.67–8. [200] *DI* 1.24.75; cf. *Sermo* XXIII.31.

language a special quality in that human-made names are not directly the product of divine artifice, rather they are in themselves the product of divine art, that is, the product of humans. As such, they have the unique capacity of integrating human cognition into the very activity of divine creation, as we can see in greater detail when we consider the process of conjecture.

Knowing

The second activity of human artifice we will consider is conjecture (coniectura). According to Cusa, 'a conjecture is a positive assertion that participates of truth as it is with a degree of otherness'.[201] The 'degree of otherness' of which Cusa writes is telling of the epistemological process. By conjectures, humans may know a measure of the truth, but not the precise truth. Conjecture is therefore a form of perspectival judgment. It is not a guess or a hunch, as the term tends to indicate in contemporary contexts. It takes from the oneness outside of itself to add to the oneness of its own reason. This agrees with the doctrine of learned ignorance; if precise truth is unattainable, then 'every human affirmation about what is true is a conjecture'.[202]

Cusa develops a contrast between the activity of the divine mind and the human mind, which both contrasts their natures, whilst also demonstrating how human conjecture participates in the divine mind. This parallel is described as follows:

> It must be the case that conjectures originate from our minds, even as the real world originates from infinite divine reason. For when, as best it can, the human mind (which is a lofty likeness of God) participates [participat] of the fruitfulness of the creating nature, it produces from itself, qua image of the omnipotent form, rational entities, in the likeness of real entities. Consequently, the human mind is the form of a conjectured world, just as the divine mind is the form of the real world. Therefore, just as that absolute divine being is all that which there is in each existing thing, so too the oneness of the human mind is the being of its own conjectures.[203]

The world as it is originates in God's mind, and the world as we know it originates in our own mind through conjecture, which remakes the world that we experience for us to know. In this way the human mind participates in the activity of the divine mind, in its 'fruitfulness', with the divine mind creating 'real entities' and the human mind 'rational entities'. God is the 'form' of the world since all substantive reality would not be without God. Similarly, the human mind is the form of a conjectured world, whereby through abstraction from perception, the human mind forms concepts which are the likenesses of

201 *DC* 1.11.57. 202 *DC* 1.1.2. 203 *DC* 1.1.5.

perceived objects, without which we would not know the world.[204] Finally, just as the divine is the ultimate being of all beings, the human mind is the ultimate being of all conjectures. The consequence of this parallel is that whilst the divine mind constitutes precise truth, the human mind holds an image or likeness of that proper truth.[205] Elsewhere, Cusa offers this in a succinct contrast that 'our mind differs from the divine mind as seeing differs from doing. The divine mind creates by conceiving; our mind assimilates by conceiving – i.e. by making concepts, or intellectual viewings. The divine mind is a reifying power; our mind is an assimilative power'.[206]

Among the various terms that Cusa employs to articulate the participatory relationship between God and creation, is the language of enfolding and unfolding. Cusa describes God's infinite mind as the 'absolute enfolding', and what is enfolded in the maximum oneness of the divine mind is unfolded in creation.[207] This is something Cusa articulates in a catalogue of contrasting enfolding and unfolding terms: oneness-multitude, rest-motion, simplicity-composition, identity-diversity, equity-inequity, and union-division.[208] For Cusa, God's unfolding in creation is the activity whereby the divine makes itself available to become intelligible for humans. Yet further steps are necessary, wherein divine unfolding is reversed as it were, into the enfolding of the human mind:

> Therefore, the actuality of our intelligence consists in its partaking of the divine Intellect. But since that most actual power can be received only with a variety-of-otherness (a variety, that is, which is received somehow concurrently with the power), it happens that the participant-minds participates of the most actual Intellect with a degree of otherness – i.e., with that degree of actuality which (in relation to the divine intellect) is otherness or potency. Therefore, it is rather the case that our entire intelligence consists of participation in the divine.[209]

Humans may not know oneness, simplicity or equity, for example, as they are in themselves. Rather we only know them in their potency and otherness, that is as multitudes, compositions and inequities. The human mind unfolds a rational world from its own act of enfolding, conjecturing by means of composition, comparison, differentiation, and abstraction.[210] In doing so 'we are elevated to a nearer likeness of this reason in proportion as we have deepened our mind, of which infinite reason is the unique vital center. This is why we aspire, by means of a natural desire, unto the perfecting branches of knowledge'.[211]

---

[204] Cf. *Sermo* CCXVI. 16–17. [205] *DM* 3.72–3. [206] *DM* 7.99. [207] *DM* 4.75.
[208] *DM* 4.75. [209] *DC* 1.11.56. [210] *DC* 1.1.5. [211] *DC* 1.1.5.

For Cusa, the nature of human knowledge is that of a continual process of conjectural artifice and participatory approximation. As was the case with names, knowledge is characterised on the one hand by the subjective perspective of the individual who conjectures it, such that 'all created minds partake of the divine mind differently and in terms of otherness-of-variation'.[212] On the other hand, that variation is necessary in itself, since 'that inaccessible loftiness is not to be approached as if there could be no access at all to it. Nor, having been approached, is that loftiness to be supposed actually to have been apprehended. Rather, that it can always be approached more closely, while it remains ever unattainable as it is'.[213] Knowledge itself cannot help but be participatory, and since its object is the maximum it also cannot help but be characterised by a kind of endless approximative journey. Creation benefits the human mind. The enfolded divine mind, unfolded in creation, is once again enfolded by human perception, which again unfolds the divine to us through conjecture, such that 'every human affirmation about what is true is a conjecture. For the increase in our apprehension of what is true is endless'.[214] The human desire to know is driven by this metaphysical and epistemological structure, which presents itself as an endless upward journey towards its infinite object.

Not only does the human mind approximate God's knowledge through continuing conjecture, but in holding knowledge in itself, the mind becomes ever more like the divine mind. The divine mind enfolds the true nature of the multiplicity of creation unfolded in the universe. In a parallel and approximative manner, the human mind enfolds created concepts and then unfolds them mentally in a conceptual universe. As humans we are the uniting source of our knowledge, providing our ideas with a cognitive oneness.[215] Like the creation of names just considered, this conjectured oneness is perspectival, based upon the arbitrary experience of the individual. Nevertheless, as all of creation is enfolded in the oneness of the divine mind, human conjectured knowledge cannot help but be participatory. Because of this, the human mind faintly and imperfectly mirrors the uniting unity of the divine mind. Whilst human knowledge may be conjectural and God's complete, as images of the divine, the conjectures of the mind humans have a measure of cognitive validity, such that Cusa is able to claim that 'the actuality of our intelligence consists in its partaking of the divine intellect'.[216] As the imago Dei, the human mind, through the activity of conjecture, makes itself, and in so doing, evermore participates in the mind of the maker.

212 *DC* 1.11.55. 213 *DC* 1.11.56. 214 *DC* 1.11.56. 215 *DM* 4,74. 216 *DC* 1.11.56.

Making

We now move from the cognitive activities of naming and knowing, to the actual participatory activity of physical making. In his dialogue, *Idiota de Mente*, Cusa considers this topic in relation to the making of a spoon. In the conversation between an orator, philosopher, and the layman spoon-maker, it is the last of these who is shown to have the greatest grasp of the participatory relationship between God and creation, and how human beings, in their most simple activities, are directly and intimately engaged in this participatory relationship. The act of the making of the spoon, and reflecting upon the creation of it, are all the layman needs to nourish both the body and the mind.[217]

For Cusa, what is particularly noteworthy about an object such as a spoon is that it is a human invention. Unlike the sculptor or painter who borrows their exemplars from the world around them, the spoon maker has no other exemplar except the idea in his own mind, as Cusa has the layman explain: 'For in my work I do not imitate the visible form of any natural object, for such forms of spoons, dishes, and jars are perfected by human artistry alone. So my artistry involves the perfecting, rather than the limiting, of created visible forms, and in this respect it is more similar to the infinite art'.[218]

According to the logic of the layman, when one depicts a person in marble, or landscape on canvas, this is an act of limiting, in that it always produces less than the object it represents. Alternatively, the idea of the spoon is something that exists in the mind of the maker alone, and its physical creation is not a limitation of an already existing nature, but the bringing of a form into physical reality. This activity is more akin to the 'infinite art' of God, which has the same pattern of bringing forms into physical reality. In the act of hewing and hollowing out his wooden spoon, the layman describes how 'I continue until in the wood there comes to be the requisite proportion, wherein the form of spoonness *shines forth* fittingly. In this way you see that in the befiguring proportion of the wood the simple and imperceptible form of spoonness shines forth, as in an image of itself'.[219] Here again we see the language of 'shining forth', which we have encountered in relation to the imperceptible nature of the infinite form which '*shines forth* as the most adequate exemplar of each in every formable thing'.[220] These exemplars are less than the infinite form, but nevertheless they make the imperceptible form perceptible. The particular spoon that the layman creates has a degree of particularity relative to the individual maker, for 'in all spoons there shines forth variously only that most simple form, shining forth to a greater degree in

[217] *DM* 2.55. [218] *DM* 2.62. [219] *DM* 2.63. Emphasis added. [220] *DM* 2.67.

one spoon and to a lesser degree in another, but not appearing in a precise way in any spoon'.[221] Here we see in terms of the creation of a physical artifact, the argument we have already encountered in relation to both names and conjectures, namely that there is one infinite name and one infinite form, and that all of the names and conjectures that are the product of human artifice variously participate in the one infinite divine name and form. The same is true in terms of the physical act of creation. Artifacts created by humans contribute to the 'perfecting . . . of created visible forms'.[222]

Artistic Making

Spoons are not Cusa's final word on the making of artifacts nor art. Later in the same dialogue the layman brings up the example of two portraits to illustrate how the real quality of art is not, as in creative art, the representation of something, nor is it, as an applied art, the artifact that it produces. In both of these cases the artifacts are judged in relation to the exemplar, such as a particular landscape or the idea of a shoe. Instead, the real quality of art is what Cusa describes as a kind of dynamic quality: 'no matter how nearly perfect an image is, if it cannot become more perfect and more conformed to its exemplar, it is never as perfect as any imperfect image whatsoever that has the power to conform itself ever more and more, without limit, to its inaccessible exemplar. For in this respect the image, as best it can, imitates infinity'.[223] In other words, what constitutes the perfection of a created artifact is not its ability to fully achieve its exemplar, which in fact is not possible, but the ability of the image to ever approximate the exemplar. In the case of applied arts, the only way this can occur is through the creation of further artifacts. There is an inherent limitation to individual artifacts, as the particular shoe, for example, cannot become more shoe-like, and indeed through use it may degrade. In the case of creative arts such infinite approximation is possible. This is something that Cusa sets out through the example of an artist who creates two self-portraits, with one described as a 'dead portrait' and the other a 'living portrait'. In the case of the former, the dead image is in fact a greater likeness of the individual, a snapshot as it were of a particular moment in the life of the artist. In the case of the latter living image, this portrait is less like the artist, but it is 'such that when stimulated to movement by its object [i.e. the artist], it could make itself ever more conformed'.[224]

---

221 *DM* 2.63. CF. *De ber.* 56, Nathan Lyons, *Signs in the Dust: A Theory of Natural Culture and Cultural Nature* (Oxford: Oxford University Press, 2019), 72–73.

222 *Comp.* 9.27. 223 *DM* 14.149. 224 *DM* 13.149.

What Cusa precisely means by the idea of a 'living portrait' is not made fully clear from the description he offers. However, the matter with which he is concerned has less to do with the depiction of the artist in the portrait, and more to do with the depiction of the artistic process as his description makes clear. He writes that 'no one doubts that the second image is the more perfect qua imitating, to a greater degree, the art of the painter. In a similar way, every mind – even ours, too, although it is created as lower than all other minds – has from God the fact that, as best it can be, it is a perfect and living image of the infinite Art'.[225] According to Cusa, the living image better imitates 'the art of the painter', that is, the painterly activity of artistic creation. Cusa then connects this to the activity of the human mind, which is as best as possible a living image of infinite art. Elsewhere, Cusa writes 'that every created thing is, as it were, a finite infinity or a created god, so that it exists in the way in which this can best occur.'[226] at our best, humans become ever more like a God, by the cognate artifice of naming and knowing, and in the physical activity of making. As a living image, the mind is 'an image which, when stimulated, can make itself always more conformed to divine art, while the preciseness of the infinite art remains always inaccessible'.[227] In the example of the ever-approximating portrait, Cusa offers an intensified version of the human as imago Dei, involved not just in the activity of making, which itself participates in the divine activity of creation, but in making an image of the self as a dynamic creator, which re-presents to ourselves our own nature as a created god, a finite infinity that is an image of divine infinity.

Romanticism and Participatory Making

Cusa's assertions concerning art and participation find strong resonance in a number of figures from the Renaissance forward, for whom the rule of artistic creation takes on particular importance. Ficino considered art to be the rousing of the god within us,[228] and Shaftesbury concluded that 'a Poet is indeed a second Maker'.[229] For Romantic period thinkers, living through a time where assertions of participatory metaphysics had become increasingly difficult in a modern immanent frame, aesthetics held out the particular capacity to represent the transcendent through its irreducible dynamism. Among the most important theorists of this position was Friedrich Schlegel (1772–1829), who elaborated an aesthetic theory based around the concept of 'Poesie'.[230] For Schlegel, Poesie had three related meanings: first, divine

225 *DM* 13.149. 226 *DI* 2.2.104. 227 *DM* 13.149.

228 Marsilio Ficino, *Opera Omnia* (Turin: Bottega d'Erasmo, 1959), 1:287.

229 Anthony Ashley Cooper Shaftesbury, *Characteristics of Men, Manners, Opinions, Times*, ed. D. den Uyl, 3 vols. (Indianapolis: Liberty Fund, 2001), 1:82–83.

230 Hampton, *Romanticism and the Re-invention of Modern Religion*, 133–56.

Poesie is the divine universal productive principle in creation; second, it is the 'elemental force of humans [Urkraft der Menschen]' in all their productive activities; and third, it is the particular aesthetic activity of humans wherein one consciously participates in creation as a secondary creator.[231] Poesie is manifest in both the laws of physical nature and the freedom of artistic creativity. As such, according to Schlegel, Poesie is capable of uniting the objective and rational with the subjective and affective, together with an intuition of the whole. All human activity, enfolded into divine Poesie, is united by this 'higher magical power [höhere Zauberkraft]'.[232] In his famous Athenaumsfragment 116, Schlegel explains that poetry has the capacity to hover above its transcendent source, simultaneously allowing us to re-present that source in the form of a particular human creation, whilst at the same time our own poetic representation of the transcendent resists our intellectual circumscription. Romantic poetry therefore 'hovers at the midpoint between the portrayed and the portrayer, free from all real and ideal self-interest, on the wings of poetic perfection'.[233] Indeed, it is the reciprocal kinship between these two forms of creative Poesis that causes individuals to constantly reach beyond themselves with the aim of finding a sense of completion. Consequently, not unlike Cusa, Schlegel asserts that life is characterised by 'play of participation [Mitteilung] and approximation [Annäherung]'.[234]

Along similar lines of Romantic thought, Samuel Taylor Coleridge argued that poetics, also broadly conceptualised as a creative activity, allowed human beings to participate directly in the creation and unfolding of the divine in a manner that sacralised aesthetic creativity. For Coleridge, the human imagination is to be understood as 'the living Power and prime Agent of all human Perception, and as a repetition of the finite mind of the eternal act of creation in the infinite I am'.[235] Much like Cusa, therefore, perception is to be understood as a kind of secondary creation, where God's creation is recreated in the mind of the perceiver. In this context, the artist then re-presents creation back to the audience in the form of their artistic creation. Hence in Coleridge, whose language echoes God's own language of self-creation in Exodus 3:14, human participation in creation is achieved through the imagination which re-performs the divine act of creation a second time. In this context, the creative artist takes on the role of a hierophant, and their art the function of a sacrament. Referring

[231] *KA* II, 285. All quotations from Schlegel are from: Friedrich Schlegel, *Kritische Friedrich-Schlegel-Ausgabe*, ed. Ernst Behler, et al. (Munich: Schöningh, 1958–2002), 35 vols.
[232] *KA* II, 284. [233] *KA* II, 315. [234] *KA* II, 285.
[235] *The Collected Works of Samuel Taylor Coleridge, Volume 7: Biographia Literaria*, ed. James Engell and W. Jackson Bate (Princeton, NJ: Princeton University Press, 1984), 1:304

back to Cusa's central insight in the *De Docta Ignorantia*, we are unable to escape ourselves through abstract speculation in order to grasp the divine absolute in itself. Yet the self, and all the world in which it finds itself, cannot help but make present, through naming, knowing and making, the participatory reality of the divine through the process of infinite approximation.

Bibliography

Aertsen, Jan, *Medieval Philosophy as Transcendental Thought: From Philip the Chancellor (ca. 1225) to Francisco Suarez* (Leiden: Brill, 2012).

Nature and Creature: Thomas Aquinas's Way of Thought (Leiden: Brill, 1988).

Annice, Sr. M., 'Historical Sketch of the Theory of Participation', *New Scholasticism*, 26 (1952): 49–79.

Aquinas, Thomas, *An Exposition of the on the Hebdomads of Boethius*, trans. Janice L. Schultz and Edward A. Synan (Washington, DC: Catholic University of America Press, 2001).

Aquinas on Creation: Writings on the 'Sentences' of Peter Lombard, Book 2, Distinction 1, Question 1, trans. Steven E. Baldner and William E. Carroll (Toronto: Pontifical Institute of Mediaeval Studies, 1997).

Commentary on the Book of Causes, prop. 2, n. 30, trans. Charles R. Hess, Richard C. Taylor, and Vincent A. Guagliardo (Washington, DC: Catholic University of America Press, 1996).

Commentary on the Metaphysics of Aristotle, trans. John Patrick Rowan (Chicago: H. Regnery, 1961).

On the Power of God: Quaestiones Disputatae de Potentia Dei, trans. Fr. Lawrence Shapcote (Westminster: Newman Press, 1952).

Selected Writings of St. Thomas Aquinas, trans. Robert P. Goodwin (Indianapolis: Bobbs-Merrill, 1965).

Summa contra Gentiles, trans. James F. Anderson, Vernon J. Bourke, Charles J. O'Neil, and Anton C. Pegis, 4 vols. (Notre Dame: University of Notre Dame Press, 1975).

Summa Theologiae, ed. David Bourke, 60 vols. (Cambridge: Cambridge University Press, 2006).

Thomas Aquinas's Quodlibetal Questions, trans. Brian Davies and Turner Nevitt (Oxford: Oxford University Press, 2020).

Aristotle, *Metaphysics, Volume I: Books 1–9*, trans. Hugh Tredennick, Loeb Classical Library (Cambridge, MA: Harvard University Press, 1933).

Metaphysics, Volume II: Books 10–14, Oeconomica, Magna Moralia, trans. Hugh Tredennick, Loeb Classical Library (Cambridge, MA: Harvard University Press, 1935).

On the Soul, Parva Naturalia, on Breath, trans. Walter S. Hett, Loeb Classical Library (Cambridge, MA: Harvard University Press, 1957).

Aspray, Silvianne, *Metaphysics in the Reformation: The Case of Peter Martyr Vermigli* (Oxford: Oxford University Press, 2021).

Augustine, *City of God*, trans. Henry Bettenson, Penguin Classics (London: Penguin Books, 1972).

Confessions, trans. Henry Chadwick (Oxford: Oxford University Press, 2008).

'Enchiridion', in *On Christian Belief*, ed. Boniface Ramsey, trans. Bruce Harbert, The Works of Saint Augustine: A Translation for the 21st Century (Hyde Park: New City Press, 2005).

Homilies on the Gospel of John 1–40, trans. Edmund Hill, The Works of Saint Augustine: A Translation for the 21st Century (Hyde Park: New City Press, 2009).

'Miscellany of Eighty-Three Questions', in *Responses to Miscellaneous Questions*, trans. Boniface Ramsey, The Works of Saint Augustine: A Translation for the 21st Century (Hyde Park: New City Press, 2008).

'True Religion', in *On Christian Belief*, ed. Boniface Ramsey, trans. Edmund Hill, The Works of Saint Augustine: A Translation for the 21st Century (Hyde Park: New City Press, 2005).

Balthasar, Hans Urs von, 'Another Ten Years: 1975', trans. John Saward, in *The Analogy of Beauty: The Theology of Hans Urs von Balthasar*, ed. John Riches (Edinburgh: T. & T. Clark, 1986), 222–33.

Glory of the Lord: A Theological Aesthetics, trans. Erasmo Leiva-Merikakis, Andrew Louth, Frances McDonagh, et al. (San Francisco: Ignatius Press, 2006).

Theo-Drama: Theological Dramatic Theory: Three Volumes, trans. Graham Harrison (San Francisco: Ignatius Press, 1988–92).

Barth, Karl, *Nein!* (Munich: Kaiser, 1934).

Billings, Todd J., *Calvin, Participation, and the Gift: The Activity of Believers in Union with Christ* (Oxford: Oxford University Press, 2007).

Bonaventure, *The Journey of the Mind to God*, trans. Philotheus Boehner (Indianapolis: Hackett, 1993).

Boulnois, Olivier, *Être et représentation: une généalogie de la métaphysique moderne à l'époque de Duns Scot (XIIIe–XIVe siècle)* (Paris: Presses Universitaires de France, 1999).

Burrell, David, *Analogy and Philosophical Language* (New Haven: Yale University Press, 1973).

Aquinas: God and Action (London: Routledge, 1979).

Caillot, Joseph, 'La grace de union selon saint Irénée', in *Penser la foi: recherches en théologie aujourd'hui: mélanges offert à Joseph Moingt*, ed. Joseph Doré and Christoph Theobald (Paris: Cerf, 1993), 395.

Canlis, Julie, 'Being Made Human: The Significance of Creation for Irenaeus's Doctrine of Participation', *Scottish Journal of Theology*, 58.4 (2005): 434–54.

Chittick, William C., 'Ibn al-'Arabl on Participating in the Mystery', in *The Participatory Turn: Spirituality, Mysticism, Religious Studies*, ed. Jorge N. Ferrer and Jacob H. Sherman (Albany: State University of New York Press, 2008), 245–64.

Clarke, William Norris, *Explorations in Metaphysics: Being-God-Person* (Notre Dame: University of Notre Dame Press, 1994).

'The Meaning of Participation in St. Thomas', in *Explorations in Metaphysics: Being, God, Persons* (Notre Dame: University of Notre Dame Press, 1994), 92–93.

'The Meaning of Participation in St. Thomas', *Proceedings of the American Catholic Philosophical Association*, 26 (1952): 147–57.

Clavier, Mark, *Eloquent Wisdom: Rhetoric, Cosmology and Delight in the Theology of Augustine of Hippo* (Belgium: Brepols, 2014).

Clement of Alexandria, 'The Stromata or Miscellanies', trans. William Wilson, in *Ante-Nicene Fathers: Volume II*, ed. Rev. Alexander Roberts and James Donaldson (New York: Burr Printing House, 1885).

Coleridge, Samuel Taylor, *The Collected Works of Samuel Taylor Coleridge, Volume 7: Biographia Literaria*, ed. James Engell and W. Jackson Bate (Princeton, NJ: Princeton University Press, 1984).

Cusanus, Nicolaus, *Nicolai de Cusa Opera Omnia jussu et auctoritate Academicae Litterarum Heidelbergensis* (Leipzig-Hamburg: Meiner, 1932–2007).

Davison, Andrew, *Participation in God: A Study in Christian Doctrine and Metaphysics* (Cambridge: Cambridge University Press, 2019).

Dillon, John and Daniel J. Tolan, 'Ideas as Thoughts of God', in *Christian Platonism: A History*, ed. Alexander J. B. Hampton and John Peter Kenney (Cambridge: Cambridge University Press, 2021), 34–52.

Dobell, Brian, *Augustine's Intellectual Conversion: The Journey from Platonism to Christianity* (Cambridge: Cambridge University Press, 2009).

Dodds, Eric Robertson, *Pagan and Christian in an Age of Anxiety: Some Aspects of Religious Experience from Marcus Aurelius to Constantine* (Cambridge: Cambridge University Press, 1968).

Dominiak, Paul Anthony, *Richard Hooker: The Architecture of Participation* (London: T&T Clark, 2019).

Edwards, Mark, *Culture and Philosophy in the Age of Plotinus* (London: Duckworth, 2006).

Fabro, Cornelio, *La nozione metafisica di partecipazione: secondo S. Tommaso d'Aquino* (Torino: Societa editrice internazionale, 1950).

Ferrer, Jorge N., 'Spiritual Knowing as Participatory Enaction: An Answer to the Question of Religious Pluralism', in *The Participatory Turn: Spirituality, Mysticism, Religious Studies*, ed. Jorge N. Ferrer and Jacob H. Sherman (Albany, NY: State University of New York Press, 2008), 135–72.

Ficino, Marsilio, *Opera Omnia* (Turin: Bottega d'Erasmo, 1959).

Ge, Yonghua, *The Many and the One: Creation as Participation in Augustine and Aquinas* (Lanham: Lexington Books, 2021).

Geiger, Louis-Bertrand, *La participation dans la philosophie de St. Thomas d'Aquin* (Paris: J. Vrin, 1942).

Gillespie, Michael Allen, *Nihilism before Nietzsche* (Chicago: University of Chicago Press, 1995).

Glouberman, Mark, *Persons and Other Things: Exploring the Philosophy of the Hebrew Bible* (Toronto: University of Toronto Press, 2021).

Hampton, Alexander J. B., 'Christian Platonism, Nature and Environmental Crisis', in *Christian Platonism: A History*, ed. Alexander J. B. Hampton and John Peter Kenney (Cambridge: Cambridge University Press, 2021), 381–407.

'God's Ideas', in *T&T Clark Encyclopedia of Christian Theology*, ed. Jana Bennett, Stephen Cone, and Jason Fout (New York: Bloomsbury, in press) .

'Nature and Aesthetics: Methexis, Mimēsis and Poiēsis', in *The Cambridge Companion to Christianity and the Environment*, ed. Alexander J. B. Hampton and Douglas Hedley (Cambridge: Cambridge University Press, 2022), 263–85.

'Platonism, Nature and Environmental Crisis', in *Christian Platonism: A History*, ed. Alexander J. B. Hampton and John Kenney (Cambridge: Cambridge University Press, 2021), 381–407.

Romanticism and the Re-invention of Modern Religion: The Reconciliation of German Idealism and Platonic Realism (Cambridge: Cambridge University Press, 2019).

Harnack, Adolf, *History of Dogma*, trans. Neil Buchanan, 7 vols. (London: Williams and Norgate, 1897).

Harrison, Peter, *The Bible, Protestantism, and the Rise of Natural Science* (Cambridge: Cambridge University Press, 1998), 45–56.

Hermann, Fritz-Gregor, 'μετ-χειν, μεταλαμβ-νειν and the Problem of Participation in Plato's Ontology', *Philosophical Inquiry*, 25.3–4 (2003): 19–56.

Honnefelder, Ludger, *Scientia Transcendens; Johannes Duns Scotus* (Munich: C. H. Beck, 2005).

Woher kommen wir? Ursprünge der Moderne im Denken des Mittelalters (Berlin: Berlin University Press, 2008).

Irenaeus, *Irénée de Lyon Contre les Hérésies: Édition Critique*, ed. Louis Doutreleau, Bertrand Hemmerdinger, Charles Mercier, et al., Sources Chrétiennes (Éditions du Cerf: Paris, 1952–82).

On the Apostolic Preaching: St Irenaeus of Lyons, trans. John Behr, Popular Patristics Series 17 (Crestwood: St Vladimir's Seminary Press, 1997).

St. Irenaeus of Lyons: Against the Heresies, trans. Dominic J. Unger, Ancient Christian Writers (Mahwah: Paulist Press, 1992–2024).

Israel, Jonathan I., *Radical Enlightenment: Philosophy and the Making of Modernity 1650–1750* (Oxford: Oxford University Press, 2001).

Justin Martyr, *The First and Second Apologies*, trans. Leslie William Barnard, Ancient Christian Writers (New York: Paulist Press, 1997).

Karamanolis, George, 'Creation in Early Christianity', in *The Routledge Handbook of Early Christian Philosophy*, ed. Mark Edwards (London: Rutledge, 2020), 56.

The Philosophy of the Early Church (New York: Abingdon, 2021).

Kenney, John Peter, *Mystical Monotheism: A Study in Ancient Platonic Theology* (Hanover: Brown University Press, 1991).

'"None Come Closer to Us than These": Augustine and the Platonists', *Religions*, 7.9 (2016): 114.

'Platonism and Christianity in Late Antiquity', in *Christian Platonism: A History*, ed. Alexander J. B. Hampton and John Peter Kenney (Cambridge: Cambridge University Press, 2021), 177–79.

The Mysticism of St Augustine: Rereading the Confessions (London: Rutledge, 2005).

Kimbrough, Steven T., *Partakers of the Life Divine: Participation in the Divine Nature in the Writings of Charles Wesley* (Eugene: Cascade, 2016).

Laertius, Diogenes, *Lives of the Eminent Philosophers*, trans. Robert Drew Hicks, Loeb Classical Library (Cambridge, MA: Harvard University Press, 1925).

Lancaster, Brian L., 'Engaging with the Mind of God: The Participatory Path of Jewish Mysticism', in *The Participatory Turn: Spirituality, Mysticism, Religious Studies*, ed. Jorge N. Ferrer and Jacob H. Sherman (Albany: State University of New York Press, 2008), 173–97.

Lyons, Nathan, *Signs in the Dust: A Theory of Natural Culture and Cultural Nature* (Oxford: Oxford University Press, 2019).

McGrath, Sean, *Thinking Nature: An Essay in Negative Ecology* (Edinburgh: Edinburgh University Press, 2019).

McInerny, Ralph, *Aquinas and Analogy* (Washington, DC: Catholic University of America Press, 1996).

Studies in Analogy (The Hague: Martinus Nijhoff, 1968).

The Logic of Analogy: An Interpretation of St. Thomas (The Hague: Martinus Nijhoff, 1961).

McIntosh, Mark Allen, *Christology from Within: Spirituality and the Incarnation in Hans Urs von Balthasar* (Notre Dame: University of Notre Dame Press, 1996).

McMullin, Ernan, 'Creation Ex Nihilo: Early History', in *Creation and the God of Abraham*, ed. David B. Burrell, Carlo Cogliati, Janet M. Soskice and William R. Stoeger (Cambridge: Cambridge University Press, 2010), 11–23.

Meconi, David V., 'St. Augustine's Early Theory of Participation', *Augustinian Studies*, 27 (1996): 83.

Minns, Denis, *Irenaeus: An Introduction* (London: T&T Clark, 2010).

Moreschini, Claudio, 'Neoplatonismo e cristianesimo: "Partecipare d Dio" secondo Boezio e Agostino', in *Sicilia e Italia suburbicaria tra IV e VIII secolo*, ed. Salvatore Pricoco, Francesca Rizzo Nervo, and Teresa Sardella (Soveria Mannelli: Rubbettino Editore, 1991), 283–95.

Moutsopoulos, Evangelos, 'L'Idée de participation: Cosmos et praxis', *Philosophia*, 32 (2002): 17–21.

Nicholas of Cusa, *De Coniecturis*, in *Nicholas of Cusa: Metaphysical Speculations: Volume Two*, trans. Jasper Hopkin (Minneapolis: A. J. Banning Press, 2000), 166–299.

De Docta Ignorantia, in *Nicholas of Cusa on Learned Ignorance: A Translation and an Appraisal of de Docta Ignorantia*, trans. Jasper Hopkins (Minneapolis: A. J. Banning Press, 1985), 54–161.

Idiota de Mente, in *Nicholas of Cusa on Wisdom and Knowledge*, trans. Jasper Hopkins (Minneapolis: A. J. Banning Press, 1996), 528–601.

Normann, Friedrich, *Teilhabe: ein Schlüsselwort der Vätertheologie* (Münster: Aschendorff, 1978).

Northcott, Michael, *God and Gaia: Science, Religion and Ethics on a Living Planet* (Abingdon: Routledge, 2023).

O'Rourke, Fran, *Pseudo-Dionysius and the Metaphysics of Aquinas* (Leiden: Brill, 1992).

Osborn, Eric F., *Irenaeus of Lyons* (Cambridge: Cambridge University Press).

Philo of Alexandria, 'On the Account of the World's Creation Given by Moses', in *Philo Volume I*, trans. George Herbert Whitaker, Loeb Classical Library (Cambridge, MA: Harvard University Press, 1929).

Pickstock, Catherine, *After Writing: On the Liturgical Consummation of Philosophy* (Oxford: Blackwell, 1997).

Plato, *Complete Works*, ed. John M. Cooper, trans. Donald J. Zeyl (Indianapolis: Hackett, 1997).

Popkin, Richard, *The History of Scepticism: From Savonarola to Bayle* (Oxford: Oxford University Press, 2003).

Przywara, Erich, *Analogia Entis: Metaphysics, Original Structure and Universal Rhythm*, trans. John R. Betz and David Bentley Hart (Grand Rapids: William B. Eerdmans, 2014).

Pseudo Dionysius, 'Divine Names', in *Pseudo-Dionysius: Complete Works*, trans. Colm Luibheid (New York: Paulist Press, 1987).

Rothberg, Donald, 'Connecting Inner and Outer Transformation: Toward an Extended Model of Buddhist Practice', in *The Participatory Turn: Spirituality, Mysticism, Religious Studies*, ed. Jorge N. Ferrer and Jacob H. Sherman (Albany: State University of New York Press, 2008), 349–70.

Runia, David T., *Philo of Alexandria and the Timaeus of Plato* (Leiden: Brill, 1968).

Schindler, David C., 'What's the Difference? On the Metaphysics of Participation in a Christian Context', *The Saint Anselm Journal*, 3.1 (2005): 1–27.

Schlegel, Friedrich, *Kritische Friedrich-Schlegel-Ausgabe*, ed. Jean-Jacques Anstett, Ernst Behler, Ursula Behler, et al., 35 vols. (Munich: Schöningh, 1958–2002).

Schmaltz, Tad M., *Radical Cartesianism: The French Reception of Descartes* (Cambridge: Cambridge University Press, 2002).

Schneewind, Jerome B., *The Invention of Autonomy: A History of Modern Moral Philosophy* (Cambridge: Cambridge University Press, 1998).

Shaftesbury, Anthony Ashley Cooper, *Characteristics of Men, Manners, Opinions, Times*, ed. Douglas den Uyl, 3 vols. (Indianapolis: Liberty Fund, 2001).

Sherman, Jacob H., 'A Genealogy of Participation', in *The Participatory Turn: Spirituality, Mysticism, Religious Studies*, ed. Jorge N. Ferrer and Jacob H. Sherman (Albany: State University of New York Press, 2008), 81–112.

'The Book of Nature', in *The Cambridge Companion to Christianity and the Environment*, ed. Alexander J. B. Hampton and Douglas Hedley (Cambridge: Cambridge University Press, 2022), 96–113.

Smyth, Herbert Weir, *Greek Grammar*, rev. Gordon Messing (Cambridge, MA: Harvard University Press, 1984).

Soskice, Janet M., 'Creatio Ex Nihilo: Jewish and Christian Foundations', in *Creation and the God of Abraham*, ed. David B. Burrell, Carlo Cogliati, Janet M. Soskice and William R. Stoeger (Cambridge: Cambridge University Press, 2010), 30–31.

Tollefsen, Torstein, *The Christocentric Cosmology of St Maximus the Confessor* (Oxford: Oxford University Press, 2008).

Törönen, Melchisedec, *Union and Distinction in the Thought of St Maximus the Confessor* (Oxford: Oxford University Press, 2007).

Tresmontant, Claude, *Études de métaphysique biblique* (Paris: J. Gabalda, 1955).

Tresmontant, Claude and Ronald Koshoshek, 'Biblical Metaphysics', *Cross Currents*, 10.3 (1960): 229–50.

Vainio, Olli-Pekk, *Justification and Participation in Christ: The Development of the Lutheran Doctrine of Justification from Luther to the Formula of Concord (1580)* (Leiden: Brill, 2008).

Velde, Rudi te, *Aquinas on God: The 'Divine Science' of the Summa Theologiae* (Aldershot: Ashgate, 2006).

Williams, Rowan, 'Creation', in *Augustine through the Ages*, ed. Allan D. Fitzgerald (Grand Rapids: William B. Eerdmans, 1999).

Wippel, John F., *The Metaphysical Thought of Thomas Aquinas: From Finite Being to Uncreated Being* (Washington, DC: Catholic University of America Press, 2000).

Young, Frances, '"Creatio Ex Nihilo": A Context for the Emergence of the Christian Doctrine of Creation', *Scottish Journal of Theology*, 44.2 (1991): 139–51.

Yovel, Jonathan, 'The Creation of Language and Language without Time: Metaphysics and Metapragmatics in Genesis 1', *Biblical Interpretation*, 20.3 (2012): 205–25.

Acknowledgements

There is much that one puts into even a small book, and there is even more given by others. In many ways, this Element is a conversation with hundreds of students I have had over the past years with whom I have explored the fascinating concept of participation as one of the constituent components of the Western social imaginary. It is with these and future students in mind, with their questions and enthusiasm, that I have written this text.

My thanks to the Social Sciences and Research Council of Canada for funding that supported the research undertaken in this project and to the University of Toronto, my academic home. I also wish to thank the University of Notre Dame Australia, where much of this text was conceived as a visiting research fellow at the new Centre for the History of Philosophy at the School for Philosophy and Theology. In particular, I wish to thank Nathan Lyons and David Bronstein for their invitation, and to offer my congratulations in establishing the new centre which will undoubtedly be the home of many research projects in the coming years.

The most important, the simplest, and the truest ideas are always the most difficult to understand or express. What is true here of participation is also true of gratitude. I have a vivid memory from my early days as a student at Cambridge, sitting in the office of Catherine Pickstock as she sketched out a diagram of participatory being. This has remained with me ever since, and I am thankful to her for planting this metaphysical seed.

My thanks to my longstanding conversation partners and friends Andrew Davison, John Kenney, and Evan King. I also wish to particularly thank two of my students at the University of Toronto, James Nowak and Martin Pinckney, whose interests and questions spurred me on to write more on participation. My sincere thanks to Shaun Blanchard and Charles Taliaferro for their considerations and questions and to Nathan Scott for his work on the manuscript. Most of all my gratitude is due to Nicole and Elspeth, to whom I dedicate this labour.

Alexander Hampton
Feast of Saint Thomas Aquinas
Niagara-on-the-Lake

Cambridge Elements ☰

History of Philosophy and Theology in the West

Alexander J. B. Hampton
University of Toronto

Alexander J. B. Hampton is a professor at the University of Toronto, specialising in metaphysics, poetics, and nature. His publications include *Romanticism and the Re-Invention of Modern Religion* (Cambridge 2019), *Christian Platonism: A History* (ed.) (Cambridge, 2021), and the *Cambridge Companion to Christianity and the Environment* (ed.) (Cambridge, 2022).

Editorial Board

About the Series

In the history of philosophy and theology, many figures and topics are considered in isolation from each other. This series aims to complicate this binary opposition, while covering the history of this complex conversation from antiquity to the present. It reconceptualizes traditional elements of the field, generating new and productive areas of historical enquiry, and advancing creative proposals based upon the recovery of these resources.

Cambridge Elements ☰

History of Philosophy and Theology in the West

Elements in the Series

The Metaphysics of Divine Participation
Alexander J. B. Hampton

A full series listing is available at: www.cambridge.org/EHPT

For EU product safety concerns, contact us at Calle de José Abascal, 56–1°,
28003 Madrid, Spain or eugpsr@cambridge.org.

www.ingramcontent.com/pod-product-compliance
Ingram Content Group UK Ltd.
Pitfield, Milton Keynes, MK11 3LW, UK
UKHW020422250720
13967UKWH00007B/2771
* 9 7 8 1 0 0 9 6 2 5 0 8 1 *